A Vegan Taste of the Middle East

Other cookbooks by Linda Majzlik published by Jon Carpenter

Party Food for Vegetarians
Vegan Dinner Parties
Vegan Baking
Vegan Barbecues and Buffets
A Vegan Taste of the Caribbean
A Vegan Taste of Italy
A Vegan Taste of India
A Vegan Taste of Mexico

A Vegan Taste
of the Middle East

Linda Majzlik

JON CARPENTER

Our books may be ordered from bookshops or (post free) from
Jon Carpenter Publishing, Alder House, Market Street, Charlbury,
England OX7 3PH

Please send for our free catalogue

Credit card orders should be phoned or faxed to 01689 870437
or 01608 811969

First published in 2002 by
Jon Carpenter Publishing
Alder House, Market Street, Charlbury, Oxfordshire OX7 3PH
☎ 01608 811969

Reprinted 2005

ISBN 1 897766 77 7

Manufactured in the UK by LPPS Ltd, Wellingborough, Northants NN8 3PJ

Contents

Breads

Desserts

Introduction

The Middle East is a vast region consisting of fifteen adjoining independent countries, all with their own distinct cultures, customs and traditions. The region is in the south-western corner of Asia and joins three continents: of Africa to the south-west, Europe to the north-west and the rest of Asia to the north and east. It is no surprise, then, that the exotic cuisine of the region consists of an eclectic mix of herby Mediterranean and spicy African and Asian flavours. Both herbs and spices are valued for their preservative and medicinal properties, and for centuries Arabs controlled the profitable spice trade, obtaining spices from other parts of Asia including the Far East.

The Bedouins who roamed the land thousands of years ago are believed to have been the first farmers in the world. Instead of living a nomadic lifestyle in search of food, they discovered that they could grow wheat and other cereal crops which would enable them to settle permanently in one area. Other ancient crops include dates and figs and both of these still feature regularly in sweet and savoury dishes. Dates, along with coffee, are traditionally offered to guests in Arab homes as a symbol of hospitality and welcome. Many different varieties of dates are grown and they are often stuffed with ground nuts or other chopped dried fruits.

Much of the region is desert with very little rainfall and overall only a small proportion of the land is under cultivation. Much of this requires irrigation, but more favourable growing conditions exist in a fertile crescent that spans parts of Jordan, Israel, Iraq, Syria and Lebanon. Cereals, vegetables, pulses, citrus and other fruits and olives grow particularly well in this area. In Israel almost half of the country's food is produced on kibbutzim, where individuals and families live and work together, sharing and alternating jobs on the farm to produce food for themselves and others. Although many foods, most notably citrus fruits, dates, figs and nuts, are exported from the region, most Middle Eastern countries need to import a high proportion of their food from other countries.

Many foods are prepared according to tradition and religious beliefs and the sharing of food is seen as a symbol of hospitality. A typical Middle Eastern meal in many homes might consist of a mezze – a selection of little savoury dishes – followed by a stew or casserole served with a grain dish and flatbread, with a sweet pastry and coffee for dessert. Coffee is always served black and is sometimes flavoured with ginger. Bread forms a very important part of the diet and it is eaten with every meal. It is also highly revered and stale bread is never wasted, but finds its way into other dishes as breadcrumbs for binding or toppings, blended in sauces, or toasted and added to salads. Soups are very popular and are served at any time of day, even for breakfast. They are also served to literally break the daily fast in the Islamic holy month of Ramadan.

With staple foods such as wheat, barley, rice and pulses being combined with vegetables, fresh and dried fruits and nuts, the basic Middle Eastern diet is altogether very healthy and one which will suit vegans admirably.

The Vegan Middle Eastern Storecupboard

A well stocked storecupboard containing basic ingredients is important to the Middle Eastern cook, as many dishes can be prepared from these alone. Other dishes simply require the addition of a selection of fresh vegetables and fruits from the vast array that are popular throughout the region.

Almonds Flaked almonds are often used as a garnish for sweet and savoury dishes and their flavour is greatly enhanced if lightly toasted before use. Ground almonds are used in various baking recipes and occasionally in savoury dishes. Almonds are rich in protein, vitamins B and E and calcium.

Apricots Dried apricots are used in a variety of dishes, both sweet and savoury, and are also blended to make delicious drinks. Apricots are rich in iron, fibre, vitamins and minerals. Choose plump, unsulphured varieties for the best flavour.

Barley Believed to be the first cultivated grain, barley is grown extensively in the Middle East and provides a staple food in many areas. Whole or pot barley is more nutritious than pearl, as it has not been stripped of nutrients in the milling process. Barley is used in soups, casseroles, stews and salads, or simply served as a grain dish either on its own or mixed with other grains and vegetables.

Beans Many varieties of beans are used throughout the region, with borlotti, butter, flageolet, ful medames and red kidney some of the most popular. Ful medames may only be available from specialist groceries. All beans are a good source of protein, fibre and minerals and it is a good idea to cook them in bulk as they freeze successfully.

Breadcrumbs These can be used for savoury toppings or for helping to bind mixtures for falafel, patties and koftas. Any type of bread can be made into crumbs by simply whizzing chunks in a food processor or nutmill. Breadcrumbs can be stored in the freezer and used from frozen.

Bulgar wheat Made from dried, crushed wheat berries which have had the bran removed, bulgar simply needs to be soaked in liquid before use. It is the main ingredient in tabbouleh – a minted salad served all over the Middle East. Bulgar is also made into kibbeh, used in savoury stuffings for vegetables or cooked like rice in pilaffs.

Capers The small green flower buds from a trailing bush, capers have a piquant taste and are sold preserved in either vinegar or brine. They are used as an ingredient and for garnishing.

Chickpeas As well as being the main ingredient in hummus and falafel, chickpeas are used regularly in stews and casseroles and made into salads. These creamy, nutty-flavoured peas combine well with all other ingredients and are a good source of protein, fibre, vitamins and minerals.

Cornflour A very fine starchy white flour milled from corn. It is sometimes known as cornstarch and is used to thicken sauces and fruit puddings.

Cornmeal Ground corn, milled in various grades from fine to coarse. The fine variety is used in the recipe for Turkish cornbread.

Dates These are probably the fruit most commonly associated with the Middle East and they are used throughout the region in both sweet and savoury dishes. Fresh and dried dates are also split, filled with a mixture of ground nuts and other dried fruits and served as part of a mezze. Dates for cooking are sold pitted and loose or pitted and compressed into blocks. Boxed dessert dates are best for stuffing or for using whole in fruit salads.

Date syrup A wholesome, runny, dark syrup made from concentrated date juice. It is used in cake recipes and can also be mixed with plain soya yoghurt to make a date-flavoured topping for serving with fruit salads.

Figs These are one of the world's oldest recorded crops and they are grown extensively in the Middle East. Fresh and dried figs are commonly served for dessert, while dried figs are used in many cake and pudding recipes. Figs are a rich source of fibre, iron and calcium. Dried figs sometimes have white sugary patches on them when purchased. This is nothing to worry about – it just means that some of the natural sugar in the figs has crystallised.

Filo pastry Widely used all through the region for sweet and savoury dishes, filo pastry is made from flour, salt and water. It is best bought, either frozen or chilled, as it is difficult and time-consuming to make. The sheets need to be brushed with either melted margarine for sweet recipes or olive oil for savoury recipes before cooking.

Flower waters Both rose and orange flower waters are used as essential flavourings in desserts, cakes, biscuits and drinks. Beware of imitations – authentic flower waters are distilled from real flowers rather than being made with chemicals.

Gherkins A variety of small cucumber, sold in jars pickled in dill-flavoured vinegar. They are used to add their distinctive sweet-sour flavour to various savoury dishes, salads and dressings.

Ground rice White rice which has been milled to a grainy powder, ground rice is used to make rice puddings and fillings for sweet pastries. It is also a main ingredient in fruited rice cake, a Middle Eastern speciality.

Hazelnuts These are grown in abundance in Turkey and are used in both sweet and savoury recipes. Skinned hazelnuts are used in the recipes here and as with all nuts they are best bought whole for grinding or chopping at home.

Herbs For strength of flavour, dried herbs are often used in preference to fresh in recipes and these should be stored in airtight jars in a cool, dark cupboard.

Basil The large aromatic leaves of the basil plant, used fresh or dried, combine particularly well with aubergines and tomatoes. Fresh whole leaves make a flavourful addition to green salads.

Bay leaves The aromatic dried leaves of an evergreen tree with a distinct, strong, slightly bitter flavour. Dried leaves have more flavour than fresh and ground bay leaves are used sparingly for a more concentrated flavour.

Chives These are occasionally used to impart their mild oniony flavour to herb dressings.

Coriander This uniquely flavoured herb is always used fresh, either as an ingredient or as a garnish. Dried coriander should be avoided as the taste bears no comparison to the fresh variety.

Dill This feathery-leafed herb has a distinctive aniseed flavour, which combines well with potatoes and cabbage.

Mint A vital herb used for flavouring numerous Middle Eastern dishes, especially tabbouleh. Dried mint is often used in preference to fresh and this is sometimes crumbled to a powder before adding to a dish. Fresh leaves are often used for garnishing or added to green salads. In Turkey a garnish is made by heating dried mint and black pepper with a little olive oil. This is then stirred into soups, stews and casseroles just before serving.

Oregano A small-leafed herb that has a natural affinity with tomatoes. It is used both fresh and dried.

Parsley This universally popular herb is used liberally, fresh or dried, in savoury dishes and it combines well with other herbs. Fresh parsley is also widely used as garnish.

Thyme A small-leafed highly aromatic herb which is added fresh or dried to various soups, stews, dips and salads. Along with oregano it is used in its dried form in the delicious Lebanese herb bread.

Lemon juice Citrus fruits are widely grown in the region and fresh lemon juice is added to countless dips, dressings, sauces and other savoury dishes to give a desired sharp flavour.

Lentils A staple food in all Middle Eastern countries, red, brown and green lentils are used extensively to make dips, soups, stews and salads. They are often mixed with vegetables and served as accompaniments, or cooked with rice in pilaffs.

Olive oil An essential oil, used for frying and in dressings, which is also a vital ingredient in various recipes for savoury dips. Olive oil is uniquely flavoured and has no substitute. Extra-virgin oil is considered to be the best and is also the most expensive. The flavours of the various types of olive oil vary considerably, depending on whether the olives were grown in a hot or a cooler climate.

Olives Green and black olives are served either plain or marinated as part of mezze. They are blended until smooth to make delicious relishes or spreads and used as an ingredient in or garnish for many other dishes.

Pasta Not immediately thought of as a typical Middle Eastern ingredient, but much of the region's cuisine is strongly influenced by other Mediterranean countries and certain pasta dishes are very popular. Spaghetti mixed with tomato sauce topped with yoghurt and breadcrumbs, then baked in the oven, is one such favourite.

Pine kernels These tiny fragrant nuts with a sweet creamy taste are the seeds of a type of pine tree that is native to the Mediterranean area. They are used in a variety of sweet and savoury dishes and their flavour is enhanced if they are lightly toasted before use.

Pistachio nuts These light-green coloured, flavourful nuts are sold in their split shells or ready shelled, either salted or unsalted. The unsalted variety is used in savoury and sweet recipes. A bowl of shelled nuts is often served as part of a mezze.

Prunes The dried fruit of a black-skinned plum, prunes are a valuable source of iron, calcium and vitamins. They are sometimes added to casseroles and mixed with other dried fruits to make fruit salads. They can be bought either stoned or unstoned and the no-need-to-soak variety is the most tender.

Rice A staple food throughout the region, rice is a good source of vitamins and minerals. White and brown long grain and basmati rices are served either simply cooked or mixed with fruits, vegetables, nuts and spices to make pilaffs.

Semolina A nutritious and versatile meal made from durum wheat, semolina is used in a host of pudding, biscuit and cake recipes. It is also mixed with flour to make a casing for ma'moul – a date-and-walnut-stuffed pastry which is served in several Middle Eastern countries.

Sesame seeds These tiny protein-packed seeds are popular in all Middle Eastern countries where they are used for garnishing, in biscuit recipes and for sprinkling on breads and pastries before baking.

Soya milk Unsweetened soya milk has been used in both sweet and savoury recipes.

Spices A whole host of spices is used to subtly enhance the flavour of the foods being cooked. As ground spices quickly go stale and lose their flavour, they are best bought in small quantities and stored in a cool dark cupboard.

Allspice Tasting of a mixture of cinnamon, cloves and nutmeg, allspice is the dried berry of a tropical evergreen tree. Unless you have a spice mill to grind the berries it is best bought ready-ground. Allspice is used in both sweet and savoury dishes.

Black pepper A universally popular seasoning for savoury dishes. Freshly ground black peppercorns are preferred.

Cardamom This pine-fragranced spice is available in three forms: as pods, seeds or ground. The pods vary in colour, but it is generally agreed that the green variety is more flavourful and aromatic. The seeds are frequently used in rice dishes and the ground spice is sometimes used in puddings.

Cayenne pepper The dried fruit of a hot red pepper. Deep red in colour and very pungent, cayenne is used to add 'heat' to a dish.

Cinnamon Used in stick or ground form, cinnamon has a warm, comforting, sweet flavour which makes it very versatile and ideal for adding to sweet and savoury dishes.

Cloves These dried buds of an evergreen tree are valued for their anaesthetic and antiseptic properties. Whole cloves are used in savoury rice dishes, while ground cloves are used in desserts and baking recipes.

Coriander The dried seed of a plant which belongs to the parsley family. Available as seeds or ground, coriander has a mild, sweet, orangey flavour and is used in sweet and savoury dishes.

Cumin Cumin has a strong earthy flavour and is used extensively both as seeds and ground in savoury dishes throughout the region.

Ginger The dried ground root has a strong, spicy but sweet flavour and is used to make gingered coffee, a drink that is very popular in many Middle Eastern countries.

Paprika This dried ground pod of a sweet red pepper adds colour and a mild sweet flavour to savoury dishes, especially those containing tomatoes or red lentils. It is sometimes sprinkled on a dish as a garnish or mixed with olive oil and drizzled over hummus.

Saffron The most expensive of all the spices available, saffron is made from the dried stigmas of a variety of crocus. Luckily only a small amount is required to impart its colour and pungent, slightly bitter, yet aromatic taste, especially to rice dishes.

Turmeric This bright-yellow spice is the powdered rhizome of a plant belonging to the ginger family. It is valued for its anti-bacterial properties and adds colour and an earthy flavour to rice and vegetable dishes.

Sun-dried tomatoes The unique and intense flavour of sun-dried tomatoes enriches dishes made from fresh tomatoes. They are also used in a Mediterranean-influenced tomato and olive flat bread. They are available dry, for reconstituting in water before use, or preserved in olive oil, ready to use.

Tahini A thick nutritious paste made from ground sesame seeds, tahini is rich in protein, calcium and B vitamins. It adds a distinctive flavour and creaminess to sauces and dips, especially hummus. Light tahini is used in the recipes here. A dark version with a stronger flavour made from roasted seeds is also available.

Tamarind purée The fruit of a large tropical tree, tamarind is used to add sourness to savoury dishes, in particular those containing tomatoes. It is usually sold in a sticky block consisting of crushed pods, which needs to be soaked in hot water to produce a purée. Jars of ready-made purée are also available.

Textured vegetable protein A nutritious and versatile soya product which readily absorbs the flavours of other ingredients used. The natural minced variety is used here for making stuffings, pies, koftas and kibbeh.

Tinned tomatoes Sometimes used in preference to fresh tomatoes when a stronger tomato flavour is desired.

Tomato purée Used to strengthen the flavour of and add colour to tomato-based dishes.

Vinegar Red and white wine vinegars are preferred and as well as being used in dressings they are sometimes added to sauces, soups and stews if an acidic taste is required.

Vegetable stock Used in a variety of savoury recipes, home-made vegetable stock is easy to make and adds a more authentic flavour than stock cubes. It can be made in bulk and frozen in measured quantities. Peel and chop a selection of vegetables such as carrots, celery, courgette, peppers, onion and potato. Put them in a pan and add a couple of chopped garlic cloves, a few sprigs of parsley and a bay leaf. Cover with water and bring to the boil. Cover the pan and simmer for 30 minutes. Strain the liquid off through a fine sieve.

Vine leaves Fresh vine leaves can be bought in specialist groceries and need to be soaked in boiling water before stuffing. Vine leaves packed in brine are more readily available and these should be thoroughly washed in warm water to remove the salt before use. As well as stuffing with savoury mixtures, vine leaves are often used to line serving platters for koftas, patties, falafel and savoury pastries.

Walnuts These are grown in several Middle Eastern countries and naturally find their way into numerous sweet and savoury dishes. Walnut pieces are cheaper to buy than walnut halves and are ideal for grinding and chopping. Walnuts have been found to have positive health benefits as they help to lower cholesterol levels in the body.

Wheat berries Husked whole wheat grains, commonly called berries, are rich in protein, vitamins and minerals. They are used in soups and salads and

made into pilaffs, either on their own or mixed with other grains. Wheat berries need to be soaked in boiled water for 2 hours before cooking.

Yeast   Easy-blend dried yeast is used in the pastry and bread recipes requiring yeast. It is simple to use as it does not need to be reconstituted in liquid.

Yoghurt This is a vital ingredient in all Middle Eastern countries. It is used in a multitude of recipes, simply served plain as a garnish and also thinned with water to make a refreshing drink. Plain soya yoghurt is an excellent substitute for the home-made variety that many Middle Eastern cooks use.

MEZZE

Instead of having just one starter, a selection of savoury dishes called mezze is commonly served as a first course in many Middle Eastern countries. They can range from simple little dishes to the more elaborate and the number of dishes offered is often seen as a symbol of the host's hospitality. Dips are very popular and are usually accompanied by raw vegetables or thin strips of flatbread. Any of the salads in the salad section can also make ideal dishes for mezze, as do bowls of pistachios, olives and dates. Dates are often split and filled with a mixture of ground nuts and chopped dried fruits. Yoghurt-based dressings can also be added to accompany the little savouries and salads.

Hummus   (Serves 4/6)

8oz/225g cooked chickpeas
2 rounded tablespoons light tahini
2 tablespoons lemon juice
1 tablespoon olive oil
1 tablespoon water
1 garlic clove, crushed
black pepper
1 teaspoon olive oil
¼ teaspoon paprika

Mash the chickpeas until smooth and combine with the tahini, tablespoonful of olive oil, lemon juice, water and garlic. Season with black pepper and spoon into a serving bowl. Mix the paprika with the teaspoonful of olive oil and drizzle over the top before serving.

Red lentil dip   (Serves 4/6)

8oz/225g red lentils
2 rounded tablespoons light tahini
2 tablespoons olive oil
1 tablespoon lemon juice
2 garlic cloves, crushed
½ teaspoon paprika
black pepper

Wash the lentils, put them in a pan of water, bring to the boil, cover and simmer for about 20 minutes until tender. Drain the lentils in a sieve over a bowl and keep 4 tablespoonfuls of the cooking liquid. Put the lentils in a mixing bowl and stir in the tahini and olive oil. Add the garlic, lemon juice, paprika and cooking liquid, then season with black pepper and mix thoroughly. Transfer to a serving bowl, cover and chill.

Baba ghanoush   (Serves 6)

2lb/900g aubergine

1 garlic clove, crushed

2 rounded tablespoons light tahini

1 tablespoon lemon juice

1 tablespoon olive oil

1 teaspoon ground cumin

black pepper

chopped black olives

Cut the aubergines in half lengthwise and put them under a hot grill, turning occasionally until the flesh is soft. Scoop out the flesh and blend it with the garlic, tahini, lemon juice, olive oil and cumin until smooth, adding a little water if necessary to make a dipping consistency. Season with black pepper and pour into a serving bowl. Cover and refrigerate until cold. Garnish with chopped black olives when serving.

Avocado dip   (Serves 4/6)

2 medium avocados

2 rounded tablespoons light tahini

2 tablespoons olive oil

2 tablespoons lemon juice

2 garlic cloves, crushed

black pepper

paprika

Peel the avocados and mash them with the lemon juice until smooth. Add the tahini, olive oil and garlic and season with black pepper. Mix very well, transfer to a serving dish and sprinkle with paprika.

Mushroom, olive and yoghurt dip   (Serves 4/6)

8oz/225g mushrooms, wiped and finely chopped

2oz/50g black olives, chopped

2 spring onions, trimmed and finely chopped

1 garlic clove, crushed

1 tablespoon olive oil

1 teaspoon dried thyme

pinch of ground bay leaves

black pepper

4 rounded tablespoons plain soya yoghurt

Heat the oil and gently fry the mushrooms, spring onions and garlic until the juices begin to run from the mushrooms. Allow to cool, then blend with the remaining ingredients until smooth. Transfer to a serving bowl, cover and chill before serving.

Date and tahini dip   (Serves 4)

4oz/100g dried dates

8 fl.oz/225ml water

2 tablespoons light tahini

2 dessertspoons lemon juice

Put the dates and water in a small pan and bring to the boil. Simmer for about 5 minutes until the dates are soft, then remove from the heat and mash them smooth with the back of a spoon. Keep in the fridge until cold. Add the tahini and lemon juice and mix until well combined.

Olivada   (Serves 4)

6oz/175g green olives

2 tablespoons olive oil

2 tablespoons lemon juice

2 garlic cloves, crushed

black pepper

Put all the ingredients in a blender and blend until smooth. Transfer to a serving bowl, cover and chill before serving.

Falafel   (Serves 6)

1lb/450g cooked chickpeas

2oz/50g breadcrumbs

1 onion, peeled

4 garlic cloves

1 round teaspoon ground cumin

1 rounded teaspoon ground coriander

2 tablespoons finely chopped fresh parsley

black pepper

olive oil

Mince the onion with the garlic and put in a mixing bowl. Grate or mash the chickpeas and add, together with the remaining ingredients apart from the olive oil. Combine thoroughly until everything binds together. Take rounded dessertspoonfuls of the mixture and roll into balls in the palm of the hand. Shallow fry the balls in hot olive oil until golden, drain on kitchen paper and serve warm.

Rice and potato patties   (Makes approx. 16)

1lb/450g potatoes, peeled

4oz/100g long grain rice

1 onion, peeled and minced

1 garlic clove, crushed

1oz/25g breadcrumbs

8 fl.oz/225ml water

½ teaspoon turmeric

1 tablespoon finely chopped fresh parsley

1 tablespoon finely chopped fresh coriander

black pepper

olive oil

Chop the potatoes into even-sized chunks and boil until tender, drain and dry off over a low heat. Mash the potatoes, add the onion, garlic, parsley and coriander, then set aside. Put the rice, water and turmeric in a pan and cook until the liquid has been absorbed and the rice is done. Add to the potato mixture together with the breadcrumbs. Season with black pepper and mix very well. Allow to cool, then take rounded dessertspoonfuls of the mixture and roll into balls. Flatten each ball slightly and put them on a plate, then cover and chill them for a couple of hours. Fry in hot olive oil for a few minutes on each side until golden. Drain on kitchen paper and serve warm.

Aubergine and walnut koftas   (Makes approx. 18)

8oz/225g aubergine, finely chopped

4oz/100g breadcrumbs

3oz/75g walnuts, grated

2oz/50g plain flour

1oz/25g natural minced textured vegetable protein

1 onion, peeled and minced

1 garlic clove, crushed

2 tablespoons olive oil

5 fl.oz/150ml water

1 rounded teaspoon ground cumin

¼ teaspoon ground cinnamon

¼ teaspoon cayenne pepper

black pepper

extra olive oil

Fry the aubergine, onion and garlic in the 2 tablespoonfuls of oil for 10 minutes. Add the vegetable protein, water, cumin, cinnamon and cayenne pepper, season with black pepper, raise the heat and cook for 5 minutes whilst stirring. Remove from the heat and add the breadcrumbs, walnuts and flour. Combine thoroughly, cover and chill for an hour. Take rounded dessertspoonfuls of the mixture and roll into balls, using damp hands. Put the balls on an oiled baking sheet and brush them with olive oil. Bake in a preheated oven at 180°C/350°F/Gas mark 4 for 30 minutes. Serve either warm or cold.

Kibbeh   (Makes 8)

shell

4oz/100g bulgar wheat

½ onion, peeled and minced

1 garlic clove, crushed

8 fl.oz/225ml boiling water

1 rounded dessertspoon dried parsley

black pepper

2oz/50g plain flour

1oz/25g ground almonds

olive oil

filling

4oz/100g carrot, scraped and grated

1oz/25g natural minced textured vegetable protein

½ onion, peeled and minced

1 garlic clove, crushed

1 dessertspoon olive oil

4 fl.oz/125ml water

1 teaspoon cumin seed

¼ teaspoon ground allspice

black pepper

Soak the bulgar wheat in the boiling water for 30 minutes. Add the onion, garlic, parsley, flour and ground almonds and season with black pepper. Mix thoroughly, then cover and leave for 30 minutes.

Meanwhile make the filling. Gently fry the carrot, onion and garlic in the dessertspoonful of olive oil until softened. Add the remaining filling ingredients and stir well. Bring to the boil and simmer for about 5 minutes until the liquid has been absorbed.

Divide the shell mixture into 8 equal portions. Roll each one into an oval, then push a finger into one end to make a hole. Make this bigger by pressing the mixture between thumb and forefinger to make it thinner, but keep the oval shape. Fill the hollow with some of the filling, then press the open end together to close it. Roll the kibbeh back into an oval if it has lost its shape. Put all of the kibbeh on a plate, cover and refrigerate for a couple of hours. Fry them in hot oil until golden, drain on kitchen paper and serve warm.

Spinach and pistachio pastries   (Makes 16)

pastry

12oz/350g plain flour

6 tablespoons olive oil

cold water

extra olive oil

sesame seeds

filling

8oz/225g fresh spinach, finely chopped

2oz/50g pistachios, grated

1 onion, peeled and finely chopped

1 garlic clove, crushed

1 dessertspoon olive oil

¼ teaspoon ground allspice

black pepper

Heat the oil for the filling and fry the onion and garlic until soft. Squeeze any water from the spinach and add the spinach to the pan. Cook for about 10 minutes until the spinach is tender, then remove from the heat and add the pistachios and allspice. Season with black pepper and mix thoroughly. Set aside and allow to cool.

Put the flour in a mixing bowl and add the 6 tablespoonfuls of oil. Mix well, then gradually add enough water to make a soft dough. Knead well and divide the dough into 16 equal pieces. Roll each piece into a circle of about 4½ inches/11.5cm. Place the circles on a flat surface and divide the filling between them, putting it neatly in the centre of each one. Fold the pastry over the filling from three sides to form triangles. Pinch the pastry together to seal and transfer the triangles to a greased baking sheet with the joins underneath. Make a couple of slits in the top of each pastry, brush the tops with olive oil and sprinkle with sesame seeds. Bake in a preheated oven at 180°C/350°F/Gas mark 4 for about 25 minutes until golden brown. Serve warm with a yoghurt dressing (see pages 75-76).

Fried garlic tomatoes   (Serves 4)

1lb/450g tomatoes, thickly sliced

2 garlic cloves, crushed

2 dessertspoons olive oil

black pepper

finely sliced spring onions

finely chopped fresh parsley

Heat the oil in a non-stick pan and add the garlic and the tomato slices. Fry the slices for a minute or two on each side, until just soft but not mushy. Transfer to a serving dish and season with black pepper. Serve warm, garnished with spring onions and fresh parsley.

Marinated olives

8oz/225g green olives

2 dried chillis

2 garlic cloves, chopped

1 tablespoon finely grated lemon peel

1 bay leaf

few sprigs of fresh thyme

olive oil

Wash the olives and put them in a lidded jar or container. Add the chillies, garlic, lemon peel, bay leaf and thyme and stir well. Cover with olive oil and put the lid on. Leave in a cool place for at least 7 days. To serve, drain the olives and put them in a serving bowl. Strain the oil and use it for cooking.

Courgettes with red pepper paste   (Serves 4)

1lb/450g courgettes, chopped

8oz/225g red pepper, ground

2 garlic cloves, crushed

1 gherkin, finely chopped

1 tablespoon olive oil

1 dessertspoon lemon juice

1 teaspoon dried oregano

½ teaspoon paprika

black pepper

finely chopped fresh parsley

Fry the ground red pepper and the garlic in the oil for 5 minutes. Add the remaining ingredients, except the parsley, and stir well. Simmer for about 10 minutes, adding a little water if necessary to prevent sticking, until the courgettes are just tender. Transfer to a serving bowl and garnish with chopped parsley. Serve either hot or cold.

Vegetable kebabs   (Makes 8)

1lb/450g prepared vegetables (e.g. aubergine, courgette, peppers, mushrooms, onion, tomato), cut into even-sized chunks

marinade

1 small onion, peeled

2 garlic cloves

1 tablespoon olive oil

1 teaspoon lemon juice

1 teaspoon tamarind purée

½ teaspoon ground cumin

¼ teaspoon paprika

¼ teaspoon ground allspice

black pepper

Blend the marinade ingredients together until smooth. Put the vegetables in a mixing bowl and add the marinade. Mix well until the vegetables are coated, then cover and keep in the fridge for about 4 hours, stirring occasionally.

Thread the vegetables onto small square skewers and cook under a hot grill for about 20 minutes, turning occasionally, until cooked.

Cauliflower and beans in tahini sauce   (Serves 4)

8oz/225g cauliflower, cut into small florets

4oz/100g cooked ful medames

1 garlic clove, crushed

1 rounded tablespoon light tahini

1 rounded tablespoon plain soya yoghurt

1 tablespoon water

1 tablespoon lemon juice

¼ teaspoon ground cumin

black pepper

paprika

Put the garlic, tahini, yoghurt, water, lemon juice and cumin in a mixing bowl, season with black pepper and combine until smooth.

Steam the cauliflower until just tender, then rinse under cold running water. Drain and add to the sauce together with the beans. Mix well, transfer to a serving bowl and sprinkle lightly with paprika. Cover and chill before serving.

Stuffed vine leaves   (Makes 16)

16 vine leaves
2oz/50g bulgar wheat
4 fl.oz/125ml boiling water
1 dessertspoon olive oil
1 onion, peeled and minced
2 garlic cloves, crushed
2oz/50g dried dates, finely chopped
1oz/25g dried apricots, finely chopped
1oz/25g pine kernels, chopped
1 teaspoon coriander seeds, crushed
¼ teaspoon ground allspice
¼ teaspoon cayenne pepper
black pepper
2 fl.oz/50ml water
1 fl.oz/25ml olive oil
1 fl.oz/25ml lemon juice
lemon wedges

Wash the vine leaves, put them in a bowl and cover them with boiling water. Leave to soak for 10 minutes, then rinse and drain. Add the bulgar to the 4 fl.oz/125ml boiling water and leave for 30 minutes. Heat the dessertspoonful of oil and fry the onion and garlic until softened. Remove from the heat and add the soaked bulgar and the dates, apricots, pine kernels, coriander seeds, allspice and cayenne pepper. Season with black pepper and mix very well.

Place the vine leaves shiny side down on a flat surface. Divide the filling evenly between the leaves, putting it neatly in the centre. Fold in the sides of each leaf, then roll them up to enclose the filling. Pack the stuffed vine leaves with the seams underneath in an oiled baking dish. Mix the 1 fl.oz/25ml oil with the water and lemon juice and spoon this over the filled leaves. Cover and bake in a preheated oven at 180°C/350°F/Gas mark 4 for 45 minutes. Allow to cool, then put in the fridge until cold. Garnish with lemon wedges and serve with a yoghurt dressing (see pages 75-76).

Roasted peppers with sun-dried tomatoes (Serves 4)

1lb/450g mixed peppers

4oz/100g ripe tomato, skinned and chopped

1oz/25g sun-dried tomato, finely chopped

1 onion, peeled and finely chopped

1 garlic clove, crushed

1 tablespoon chopped capers

1 tablespoon olive oil

3 tablespoons water

1 teaspoon lemon juice

½ teaspoon dried thyme

black pepper

chopped fresh parsley

Soak the sun-dried tomatoes in the water for 2 hours. Put the peppers on a baking tray and place them under a hot grill, turning occasionally, until the skins blister. Allow to cool slightly, then remove the skins, stalks, membranes and pips and chop the flesh.

Heat the oil and gently fry the onion and garlic until soft. Add the fresh and sun-dried tomato and any remaining liquid, together with the lemon juice and thyme. Season with black pepper and stir well. Bring to the boil, cover and simmer, stirring occasionally, for 5 minutes. Add the pepper flesh and the capers and stir well. Continue simmering, stirring frequently, for 10 minutes until the mixture is thick. Spoon into a serving bowl and garnish with fresh chopped parsley. Serve either warm or cold.

Aubergine, tomato and pine kernel rolls   (Makes 6)

10oz/300g packet filo pastry

olive oil

sesame seeds

filling

12oz/350g aubergine, finely chopped

6oz/175g tomato, skinned and chopped

2oz/50g pine kernels, chopped

1 onion, peeled and finely chopped

1 garlic clove, crushed

2 tablespoons olive oil

1 dessertspoon tomato purée

½ teaspoon dried oregano

½ teaspoon dried basil

black pepper

Heat the oil for the filling and gently fry the aubergine, onion and garlic for 10 minutes, stirring frequently to prevent sticking. Add the tomato, tomato purée, oregano and basil and season with black pepper. Stir well and simmer for 5 minutes until the tomatoes become pulpy and the mixture thickens. Remove from the heat and stir in the pine kernels.

Carefully put the filo sheets on a flat surface, brushing between each one with olive oil. Cut this stack of filo sheets into 3 equal portions and halve each one to give 6 rectangles.

Divide the filling between the rectangles, placing it in the middle on the lower half of the pastry. Fold the two long edges over the filling, then roll the pastry up to enclose it. Transfer the rolls to an oiled baking sheet, brush them with olive oil and sprinkle with sesame seeds. Bake in a preheated oven at 180°C/350°F/Gas mark 4 for about 25 minutes until golden brown. Serve warm with a yoghurt dressing (see pages 75-76).

SOUPS

Soup can simply be served as a light meal at any time of day or made into a more substantial meal by adding a grain dish, flatbread and a salad. In some countries soups are garnished with sizzling olive oil in which some dried mint or other herbs and garlic have been briefly fried. During Ramadan, the Islamic holy month, a nourishing bowl of soup, usually made from grains, pulses and vegetables, is often served at sunset to break the daily fast.

Vegetable and lentil soup   (Serves 4)

1lb/450g mixed prepared vegetables (e.g. courgette, broccoli,
    cauliflower, peppers, mushrooms, carrots), chopped

14oz/400g tin chopped tomatoes

4oz/100g red lentils

1 onion, peeled and chopped

1 celery stick, trimmed and finely sliced

1 garlic clove, crushed

1 tablespoon olive oil

18 fl.oz/550ml water

1 dessertspoon tomato purée

1 dessertspoon red wine vinegar

1 bay leaf

¼ teaspoon cayenne pepper

1 rounded teaspoon dried thyme

1 rounded teaspoon dried parsley

1 rounded teaspoon dried mint

black pepper

fresh mint leaves

Heat the oil in a large pan and soften the onion, celery and garlic. Add the lentils, water, tomato purée, bay leaf, cayenne pepper, thyme, parsley and dried mint. Season with black pepper and stir well. Cover and simmer for 15 minutes, stirring occasionally, then put in the vegetables and chopped tomatoes and stir well. Bring back to the boil, cover and simmer for about 20 minutes until the vegetables are tender, stirring occasionally to prevent sticking. Stir in the vinegar, then ladle into bowls and garnish each bowl with fresh mint leaves.

Jerusalem artichoke soup   (Serves 4)

1lb/450g Jerusalem artichokes, scraped and chopped

1 onion, peeled and chopped

1 celery stick, trimmed and sliced

1 dessertspoon olive oil

1 rounded tablespoon finely chopped fresh parsley

1 dessertspoon lemon juice

black pepper

26 fl.oz/775ml vegetable stock or water

plain soya yoghurt

Gently fry the onion and celery in the oil until softened. Add the artichokes, parsley and stock and season with black pepper. Bring to the boil, cover and simmer for about 15 minutes until the vegetables are done. Allow to cool slightly, then liquidise until smooth. Return to the cleaned pan, add the lemon juice and reheat. Garnish each bowl of soup with a swirl of yoghurt when serving.

Almond and potato soup   (Serves 4)

8oz/225g potato, peeled and diced

2oz/50g ground almonds

1 onion, peeled and chopped

1 dessertspoon olive oil

black pepper

24 fl.oz/725ml vegetable stock or water

2 rounded tablespoons plain soya yoghurt

toasted flaked almonds

Heat the oil and fry the onion until soft. Add the potato, ground almonds and stock and season with black pepper. Stir well and bring to the boil, then cover and simmer for about 15 minutes until the potato is cooked. Allow to cool slightly and liquidise until smooth. Return the soup to the rinsed out pan and add the yoghurt. Stir until well combined, then slowly reheat. Serve each bowl of soup garnished with toasted flaked almonds.

Broad bean and yoghurt soup   (Serves 4)

1lb/450g shelled broad beans

1 onion, peeled and chopped

1 dessertspoon olive oil

30 fl.oz/900ml vegetable stock or water

1 teaspoon dried thyme

1 bay leaf

black pepper

4 rounded tablespoons plain soya yoghurt

Blanch the broad beans in boiling water for 1 minute. Drain and rinse under cold running water, then slip the skins from the beans and discard. Fry the onion in the oil until softened. Add the beans, stock, thyme and bay leaf and season with black pepper, stir well and bring to the boil. Cover and simmer for about 15 minutes until the beans are tender. Allow to cool slightly, then liquidise until smooth. Pour back into the cleaned pan and stir in the yoghurt. Reheat and serve.

Red lentil soup   (Serves 4)

4oz/100g red lentils

4oz/100g ripe tomato, skinned and chopped

1 large onion, peeled and chopped

2 garlic cloves, crushed

½ red chilli, finely chopped

2 dessertspoons olive oil

22 fl.oz/650ml vegetable stock or water

2 tablespoons finely chopped fresh parsley

½ teaspoon paprika

black pepper

1 dessertspoon lemon juice

Fry the onion, garlic and chilli in 1 dessertspoonful of olive oil until soft. Add the tomato and cook until pulpy. Now add the lentils, stock, parsley and paprika, season with black pepper, stir well and bring to the boil. Cover and simmer, stirring occasionally, for about 25 minutes until the lentils are soft. Allow to cool slightly, then liquidise until smooth. Return to the rinsed out pan and reheat. Mix the remaining olive oil with the lemon juice and stir into the soup just before serving.

Aubergine and wheat berry soup   (Serves 4)

8oz/225g aubergine, diced

4oz/100g wheat berries

1 onion, peeled and chopped

2 garlic cloves, crushed

1 small red chilli, finely chopped

2 tablespoons olive oil

14oz/400g tin chopped tomatoes

10 fl.oz/300ml water

1 dessertspoon tomato purée

1 rounded teaspoon dried basil

½ teaspoon paprika

1 bay leaf

black pepper

chopped fresh parsley

Put the wheat berries in a bowl and cover with boiling water. Leave to soak for 2 hours, then drain and put in a pan with clean water. Bring to the boil, cover and simmer for 1 hour, topping up with more water when necessary. Drain and set aside.

Heat the oil and fry the aubergine, onion, garlic and chilli for 10 minutes. Add the wheat berries and the remaining ingredients apart from the parsley and stir well. Bring to the boil, cover and simmer for 30 minutes, stirring occasionally to prevent sticking. Garnish each bowl of soup with chopped parsley when serving.

Bulgar, bean and pepper soup   (Serves 4)

4oz/100g bulgar wheat

4oz/100g ripe tomato, skinned and chopped

4oz/100g red pepper, ground

4oz/100g green pepper, chopped

4oz/100g mixed cooked beans

1 onion, peeled and finely chopped

1 garlic clove, crushed

½ red chilli, ground

1 tablespoon olive oil

1 dessertspoon tomato purée

1 dessertspoon red wine vinegar

1 teaspoon cumin seed

½ teaspoon paprika

black pepper

25 fl.oz/750ml water

finely chopped fresh coriander

Put the red pepper, tomato, onion, garlic, chilli and oil into a large pan and cook for about 5 minutes, stirring occasionally, until the onion is softened. Add the bulgar, green pepper, cumin seed, paprika, tomato purée and water and season with black pepper. Stir well and bring to the boil, then cover and simmer for 10 minutes. Add the beans and vinegar, stir well and continue simmering for another couple of minutes. Garnish each bowl of soup with chopped coriander.

Celeriac and orange soup   (Serves 4)

1lb/450g celeriac, peeled and diced

4oz/100g leek, trimmed and sliced

22 fl.oz/650ml vegetable stock or water

5 fl.oz/150ml fresh orange juice

1 dessertspoon olive oil

½ teaspoon coriander seeds, crushed

½ teaspoon paprika

black pepper

finely grated orange peel

Fry the leek in the oil until softened. Add the remaining ingredients except the grated peel and stir well. Bring to the boil, cover and simmer for about 15 minutes until the celeriac is tender. Allow to cool slightly and liquidise until smooth, then return to the cleaned pan and reheat. Serve in bowls garnished with grated orange peel.

Sun-dried tomato and vegetable soup   (Serves 4)

1lb/450g ripe tomatoes, skinned and chopped

8oz/225g courgette, chopped

8oz/225g yellow pepper, chopped

4oz/100g mushrooms, wiped and chopped

1½oz/40g sun-dried tomato, finely chopped

1 red onion, peeled and finely chopped

2 garlic cloves, crushed

1 tablespoon olive oil

16 fl.oz/475ml boiling water

1 bay leaf

2 teaspoons dried oregano

½ teaspoon paprika

black pepper

1 dessertspoon lemon juice

finely chopped fresh parsley

Soak the sun-dried tomato in the boiling water for 1 hour. Heat the oil and gently fry the onion and garlic. Add the fresh tomatoes and cook until pulpy. Stir in the soaked sun-dried tomato and remaining water together with the courgette, yellow pepper, mushrooms, bay leaf, oregano and paprika. Season with black pepper and stir well. Bring to the boil, cover and simmer for 15-20 minutes until the vegetables are done. Stir in the lemon juice and serve each bowl of soup garnished with chopped parsley.

Butter bean and barley soup   (Serves 4)

8oz/225g cooked butter beans

8oz/225g leek, trimmed and sliced

8oz/225g potato, scraped and diced

4oz/100g carrot, scraped and diced

2oz/50g pot barley

1 garlic clove, crushed

1 tablespoon olive oil

1 teaspoon dried thyme

1 teaspoon dried mint

1 bay leaf

black pepper

chopped fresh parsley

Put the barley in a saucepan, cover with boiling water and leave to soak for 1 hour, then put the pan on the heat and bring to the boil. Cover and simmer briskly for 30 minutes. Drain over a bowl and make the cooking liquid up to 24 fl.oz/725ml with water.

Heat the oil and fry the leek and garlic for 5 minutes. Add the liquid, barley and remaining ingredients apart from the butter beans and fresh parsley, stir well and bring to the boil. Cover and simmer for 25 minutes, stirring occasionally. Add the butter beans and continue simmering for another couple of minutes. Garnish each bowl of soup with chopped parsley.

MAIN COURSES

Spiced or herb-flavoured stews and casseroles made from tasty and nutritious combinations of vegetables, lentils, beans, dried fruits and nuts are popular main course dishes throughout the region and they are usually served with bread and a grain dish. Stuffed vegetables, which have become popular in many other cuisines around the world, are believed to have originated in the Middle East and here all manner of vegetables are expertly filled with savoury mixtures. Many types of pasta are used and these dishes are often baked with a yoghurt and breadcrumb topping or served with sauces which are distinctively flavoured with Middle Eastern herbs and spices.

Aubergine and lentil stew   (Serves 4)

1lb/450g aubergine, diced

6oz/175g brown lentils

2oz/50g dried dates, finely chopped

1 onion, peeled and chopped

2 garlic cloves, crushed

1 small red chilli, finely chopped

4 tablespoons olive oil

1 rounded teaspoon ground cumin

¼ teaspoon ground cinnamon

black pepper

chopped walnuts

Soak the lentils in water for 1½ hours. Drain and put in a pan with fresh water. Bring to the boil, cover and simmer briskly for 20 minutes. Drain, keep the cooking liquid and make this up to 18 fl.oz/550ml with water, if necessary.

Heat the oil in a large pan and gently fry the aubergine, onion, garlic and chilli for 10 minutes. Add the lentils, cooking liquid, dates, cumin and cinnamon and season with black pepper. Stir well and bring to the boil. Cover and simmer for about 25-30 minutes, stirring occasionally, until tender. Garnish with chopped walnuts and serve with warm bread and a savoury grain dish.

Chickpea and vegetable stew   (Serves 4)

14oz/400g tin crushed tomatoes

8oz/225g cooked chickpeas

8oz/225g courgette, chopped

4oz/100g carrot, scraped and finely chopped

4oz/100g red pepper, chopped

2oz/50g mushrooms, wiped and sliced

1 onion, peeled and finely chopped

2 garlic cloves, crushed

1 tablespoon olive oil

1 tablespoon tomato purée

3 tablespoons finely chopped fresh parsley

1 teaspoon dried thyme

1 teaspoon red wine vinegar

black pepper

Gently fry the onion and garlic in the oil until soft. Add the remaining ingredients and stir well. Bring to the boil, then cover and simmer gently for about 30 minutes until the vegetables are cooked and the mixture is thick. Stir occasionally to prevent sticking. Serve with warm bread and a savoury grain dish.

Potato and ful medame casserole   (Serves 4)

1½lb/675g potatoes, peeled and diced

12oz/350g cooked ful medames

6oz/175g prunes, stoned and finely chopped

6oz/175g mushrooms, wiped and sliced

6oz/175g carrot, scraped and chopped

1 onion, peeled

2 garlic cloves

1 red chilli

1 tablespoon olive oil

25 fl.oz/750ml vegetable stock

2 teaspoons ground coriander

2 teaspoons ground cumin

1 teaspoon paprika

black pepper

4 rounded tablespoons plain soya yoghurt

chopped fresh coriander

Mince the onion with the garlic and chilli, then fry in the oil until golden. Add the potatoes and spices and stir around for 1 minute. Now add the ful medames, prunes, mushrooms, carrot and stock and bring to the boil. Cover and simmer for 5 minutes. Transfer to a casserole dish and spoon the yoghurt on top. Cover and bake in a preheated oven at 180°C/350°F/Gas mark 4 for 45 minutes. Garnish with fresh coriander and serve with plain brown rice and bread.

Hazelnut, squash and chickpea casserole (Serves 4)

1½lb/675g butternut squash, peeled and diced

8oz/225g carrot, scraped and chopped

8oz/225g cooked chickpeas

2oz/50g hazelnuts, ground

2oz/50g dried dates, finely chopped

1 onion, peeled and finely chopped

1 dessertspoon olive oil

2 rounded teaspoons ground coriander

2 rounded teaspoons ground cumin

¼ teaspoon cayenne pepper

black pepper

18 fl.oz/550ml water

topping

2oz/50g breadcrumbs

1oz/25g hazelnuts, chopped

Fry the onion in the oil in a large pan. Add the spices and stir around for 30 seconds. Put in the squash, carrot, dates and water and stir well, then bring to the boil, cover and simmer for 5 minutes. Remove from the heat and stir

in the chickpeas and ground hazelnuts. Transfer to a greased shallow casserole dish.

Mix the breadcrumbs with the chopped hazelnuts and spread evenly on top. Cover and bake in a preheated oven at 180°C/350°F/Gas mark 4 for 25 minutes, then uncover and bake for another 5-10 minutes until golden brown. Serve with vegetable or salad accompaniments.

Layered bulgar and spinach bake   (Serves 4)

8oz/225g bulgar wheat

16 fl.oz/475ml water

4oz/100g red pepper

1 onion, peeled

1 tablespoon olive oil

1 rounded teaspoon dried mint

¼ teaspoon cayenne pepper

black pepper

spinach layer

8oz/225g fresh spinach, finely shredded

4oz/100g mushrooms, wiped and chopped

1oz/25g walnuts, grated

1 onion, peeled and finely chopped

1 garlic clove, crushed

2 rounded tablespoons plain soya yoghurt

1 tablespoon olive oil

¼ teaspoon ground allspice

black pepper

to serve

green salad leaves

fresh mint leaves

First make the bulgar layer. Mince the red pepper and onion and fry in the oil for 10 minutes. Add the bulgar, water, mint and cayenne pepper, season with black pepper and stir well. Bring to the boil, then remove from the heat, cover and leave for 1 hour.

Heat the oil for the spinach layer and fry the onion and garlic until softened. Add the mushrooms and fry until the juices begin to run. Put in the spinach after squeezing any water from it and cook for 15 minutes, stirring occasionally, until it is done. Remove from the heat and add the walnuts, yoghurt and allspice. Season with black pepper and mix well.

Stir the bulgar mixture and spoon half of it into a base-lined and greased 10 x 8 inch/25 x 20cm baking tin. Press down firmly and evenly, then spread the spinach mixture on top. Finish with the remaining bulgar and again press down firmly and evenly. Cover and bake in a preheated oven at 180°C/350°F/Gas mark 4 for 30 minutes, then uncover and bake for a further 10 minutes until browned. Run a sharp knife around the edges, invert onto a serving platter and carefully remove the base lining. Arrange some mixed salad leaves around the edges and garnish with fresh mint leaves. Serve with vegetables.

Stuffed baked peppers   (Serves 4)

4 peppers (each approx. 6oz/175g)

chopped fresh coriander leaves

filling

8oz/225g long grain rice

1oz/25g sultanas

1oz/25g pine kernels

1 onion, peeled and minced

2 garlic cloves, crushed

1 dessertspoon olive oil

20 fl.oz/600ml water

½ teaspoon turmeric

6 cardamom pods, husked and the seeds separated

1 inch/2.5cm stick of cinnamon, crumbled

black pepper

Cut the peppers in half and remove the stalks, membranes and seeds. Blanch in boiling water for 2 minutes, drain and put the halves in a greased baking dish. Fry the onion and garlic in the oil until soft, then add the spices and rice and stir around for 1 minute. Now add the water and sultanas and stir well. Bring to the boil, cover and simmer gently until the liquid has been absorbed and the rice is cooked. Stir in the pine kernels, then fill each pepper half with some of the filling. Cover and bake in a preheated oven at 180°C/350°F/Gas mark 4 for 30 minutes. Garnish with chopped coriander and serve with a vegetable dish.

Stuffed baked aubergine   (Serves 4)

2 aubergines (each approx. 10oz/300g)

8oz/225g mushrooms, wiped and finely chopped

2oz/50g natural minced textured vegetable protein

2oz/50g pine kernels, grated

1 onion, peeled and finely chopped

2 garlic cloves, crushed

4 tablespoons olive oil

extra olive oil

10 fl.oz/300ml vegetable stock

¼ teaspoon ground allspice

black pepper

plain soya yoghurt

chopped fresh coriander leaves

Cut the aubergines in half lengthwise and scoop out the flesh, leaving the shells about ¼ inch/5mm thick. Finely chop the flesh and fry with the onion and garlic in the 4 tablespoonfuls of oil for 10 minutes. Add the mushrooms and fry for 3 minutes more. Now add the vegetable protein, stock and allspice and season with black pepper. Simmer for about 10 minutes until the liquid has been absorbed and the mixture is thick. Remove from the heat, add the grated pine kernels and mix thoroughly. Brush the aubergine shells inside and out with olive oil and put them in a baking dish. Fill each shell with some of the filling, cover and bake in a preheated oven at 180°C/350°F/Gas mark 4 for 45 minutes. Uncover and bake for a further 5 minutes until golden brown. Garnish with yoghurt and chopped coriander and serve with vegetable and salad accompaniments.

Stuffed baked cabbage   (Serves 4)

16 large cabbage leaves

chopped fresh coriander leaves

filling

6oz/175g bulgar wheat

6oz/175g mushrooms, wiped and finely chopped

2oz/50g walnuts, grated

1 onion, peeled and grated

2 garlic cloves, crushed

12 fl.oz/350ml boiling water

2 rounded tablespoons finely chopped fresh parsley

1 dessertspoon olive oil

¼ teaspoon ground allspice

black pepper

sauce

12oz/350g ripe tomatoes, skinned and chopped

1 small red chilli, finely chopped

1 garlic clove, crushed

1 dessertspoon olive oil

2 tablespoons water

1 dessertspoon tomato purée

1 teaspoon red wine vinegar

black pepper

Soak the bulgar in the boiling water for 20 minutes. Heat the oil for the filling and fry the onion and garlic until golden. Add the mushrooms and fry until the juices begin to run, then remove from the heat and add the walnuts, parsley and allspice. Put the bulgar in a sieve and press out excess liquid with the back of a spoon. Add the bulgar to the filling mixture, season with black pepper and mix thoroughly.

Bring a large pan of water to the boil, put in the cabbage leaves and simmer for 5 minutes. Drain and remove any thick stalks. Spread the leaves out flat and divide the filling equally between them. Roll each leaf up to enclose the filling and put them in a greased shallow baking dish.

Heat the oil for the sauce and gently fry the chilli and garlic. Add the remaining sauce ingredients and stir well. Bring to the boil, cover and simmer gently for 10-15 minutes until the tomatoes are pulpy and the sauce thickens. Mash the tomatoes with the back of a spoon, then pour the sauce evenly over the stuffed cabbage leaves. Cover and bake in a preheated oven at 180°C/350°F/Gas mark 4 for 30 minutes. Garnish with chopped fresh coriander leaves and serve with salad.

Pasta with green lentil and courgette sauce (Serves 4)

8oz/225g tagliatelle or pasta shapes

sauce

8oz/225g green lentils

1lb/450g courgettes, chopped

1 onion, peeled and chopped

1 green chilli, finely chopped

2 garlic cloves, crushed

1 dessertspoon olive oil

1 rounded teaspoon ground coriander

1 rounded teaspoon ground cumin

black pepper

2 tablespoons plain soya yoghurt

chopped black olives

finely chopped fresh coriander

Soak the lentils in water for 1 hour, then drain and bring to the boil in a fresh pan of water. Cover and simmer briskly for 20 minutes. Drain over a bowl and keep the cooking liquid.

Heat the oil in a large pan and fry the onion, chilli and garlic until softened. Add the courgette, ground coriander, cumin, lentils and 16 fl.oz/475ml of the cooking liquid, making it up with water if necessary. Season with black pepper and stir well. Bring to the boil, cover and simmer for about 15 minutes, stirring occasionally, until the courgette and lentils are done. Meanwhile, cook the pasta until just tender. Drain and add to the sauce, together with the yoghurt. Stir until well combined and heated through. Garnish with chopped olives and coriander and serve with bread and a salad.

Baked spaghetti in tomato and vegetable sauce

(Serves 4)

6oz/175g spaghetti

sauce

14oz/400g tin chopped tomatoes

8oz/225g courgette, chopped

6oz/175g cooked borlotti beans

4oz/100g red pepper, chopped

4oz/100g green pepper, chopped

1 onion, peeled and chopped

2 garlic cloves, crushed

1 tablespoon olive oil

1 tablespoon tamarind purée

6 fl.oz/175ml water

2 teaspoons dried thyme

2 teaspoons dried mint

1 teaspoon paprika

black pepper

topping

6 fl.oz/175ml plain soya yoghurt

2oz/50g breadcrumbs

1oz/25g vegan 'cheese', grated

1oz/25g walnuts, finely chopped

Heat the oil in a large pan and fry the onion and garlic until soft. Add the remaining sauce ingredients and stir well. Bring to the boil, cover and simmer for 10-15 minutes, stirring occasionally, until the vegetables are just tender.

Break the spaghetti into 3 inch/8cm lengths, then cook in boiling water until just done. Drain and add to the sauce. Mix well, transfer to a greased baking dish and spoon the yoghurt evenly on top. Mix the breadcrumbs with the grated 'cheese' and walnuts and sprinkle over the yoghurt. Cover and bake in a preheated oven at 180°C/350°F/Gas mark 4 for 30 minutes, then bake uncovered for 5 minutes more until golden. Serve with a salad.

Savoury pine kernel flat pies   (Serves 4)

bases

8oz/225g plain flour

1 teaspoon easy-blend yeast

½ teaspoon salt

approx. 5 fl.oz/150ml warm water

olive oil

topping

4oz/100g carrot, peeled and grated

2oz/50g red pepper, finely chopped

1oz/25g natural minced textured vegetable protein

1oz/25g pine kernels, grated

1 onion, peeled and minced

1 garlic clove, crushed

1 tablespoon olive oil

1 rounded tablespoon plain soya yoghurt

7 fl.oz/200ml water

1 teaspoon ground cumin

¼ teaspoon cayenne pepper

black pepper

pine kernels

Mix the flour, yeast and salt in a large bowl and gradually add the water until a soft dough forms. Knead well and return to the bowl. Cover and leave in a warm place for 1 hour until risen. Knead again, then divide the dough into 4 equal pieces. Roll each piece into a ball, then roll out into a circle measuring 6 inches/15cm in diameter. Put the circles on a greased baking sheet, cover and leave in a warm place for 30 minutes.

Heat the oil for the topping and gently fry the onion and garlic for 3 minutes. Add the carrot and fry for another 3 minutes. Now add the vegetable protein, red pepper, water, cumin and cayenne pepper, season with black pepper and stir well. Bring to the boil, cover and simmer for about 15 minutes, stirring occasionally, until the liquid has been absorbed. Remove from the heat, stir in the grated pine kernels and yoghurt and mix well.

Brush the tops of the bases with olive oil, divide the filling equally between them, spreading it out evenly, and sprinkle pine kernels on top. Bake in a preheated oven at 180°C/350°F/Gas mark 4 for 20 minutes. Serve hot with vegetable accompaniments.

Spiced vegetable pie   (Serves 4/6)

pastry

8oz/225g plain flour

1 teaspoon easy-blend yeast

½ teaspoon salt

2 tablespoons olive oil

approx. 4 fl.oz/125ml warm water

soya milk

sesame seeds

filling

1lb/450g butternut squash, peeled and chopped

12oz/350g celeriac, peeled and chopped

2oz/50g dried apricots, finely chopped

1oz/25g natural minced textured vegetable protein

1oz/25g walnuts, grated

1 onion, peeled and finely chopped

1 garlic clove, crushed

1 tablespoon olive oil

4 cardamoms, husked and the seeds separated

½ teaspoon ground coriander

¼ teaspoon ground cinnamon

¼ teaspoon paprika

black pepper

12 fl.oz./350ml vegetable stock or water

Mix the flour with the yeast and salt, add the oil and stir well. Gradually add the water until a soft dough forms. Knead thoroughly, then leave in a warm place for 1 hour to rise.

Heat the oil for the filling and soften the onion and garlic. Add the remaining filling ingredients apart from the walnuts and stir well. Bring to the boil, cover and simmer, stirring occasionally, for 10 minutes. Uncover and simmer for 10 minutes more, stirring occasionally to prevent sticking, until the mixture is thick and the vegetables are cooked. Remove from the heat, stir in the walnuts and allow to cool.

Knead the dough again, then roll it out on a floured board into a 13 inch/33cm circle. Spoon the cooled filling onto the centre of the pastry, leaving a 3 inch/8cm pastry edge. Fold the pastry up over the filling, stretching it if necessary to enclose the filling completely. Invert the pie onto a greased baking sheet so that the join is underneath. Score the top with a sharp knife into diamond shapes and prick the centre of each diamond with the knife. Brush the top of the pie with soya milk and sprinkle it with sesame seeds, then bake it in a preheated oven at 180°C/350°F/Gas mark 4 for 30 minutes until golden brown. Cut into wedges and serve hot with vegetable and salad accompaniments.

Spinach, courgette and walnut borek   (Serves 4)

10oz/300g packet filo pastry, thawed

olive oil

sesame seeds

filling

1lb/450g fresh spinach

8oz/225g courgette, grated

4oz/100g green pepper, finely chopped

2oz/50g walnuts, grated

1oz/25g vegan white 'cheese', grated

1 onion, peeled and finely chopped

1 garlic clove, crushed

1 tablespoon olive oil

1 dessertspoon dried parsley

¼ teaspoon ground allspice

black pepper

Wash the spinach and put it in a large pan with only the water that clings to the leaves. Cook gently until tender, drain and allow to cool and then squeeze out any excess water. Chop the spinach finely. Heat the oil and fry the onion and garlic until soft. Add the courgette and green pepper and fry for another 2 minutes. Remove from the heat and add the spinach and remaining filling ingredients. Mix very well and allow to cool.

Cut the filo sheets in half on a flat surfacef. Place a third of the sheets on an oiled baking sheet, brushing between each sheet with olive oil. Spread half of the filling on the pastry, leaving a gap around the edges for tucking in. Repeat these two layers and finish with the remaining filo sheets. Tuck the edges under to enclose the filling and brush the top with oil. Sprinkle with sesame seeds and bake in a preheated oven at 180°C/350°F/Gas mark 4 for about 25 minutes until golden. Serve hot with vegetable and salad dishes.

GRAINS

Rice, wheat and barley are widely grown in the more fertile parts
of the region and are all staple ingredients in the Middle Eastern diet.
Pilaffs are a traditional speciality and can be made from any type of rice,
bulgar, whole wheat berries, barley or a combination of these. Plainly
cooked or more elaborate grain dishes make excellent accompaniments
for casseroles, soups and stews, whilst pilaffs can be served with bread
and salads as main courses.

Herbed barley with brown rice   (Serves 4)

4oz/100g pot barley

4oz/100g long grain brown rice

1 onion, peeled and finely chopped

1 garlic clove, crushed

1 dessertspoon olive oil

1 bay leaf

4 rounded tablespoons finely chopped fresh herbs (e.g. oregano,
thyme, parsley)

black pepper

fresh parsley sprigs

Soak the barley in water for an hour, then bring to the boil and simmer for 30 minutes. Drain and keep the cooking liquid. Pour this into a measuring jug and make up to 20 fl.oz/600ml with water.

Gently fry the onion and garlic in the oil until softened. Add the rice, barley, bay leaf, chopped herbs and cooking liquid. Season with black pepper and stir well. Bring to the boil, cover and simmer until the liquid has been absorbed and the rice and barley are cooked. Spoon into a warmed serving dish and garnish with fresh parsley sprigs.

Apricot and almond rice   (Serves 4)

8oz/225g long grain rice

2oz/50g dried apricots, finely chopped

1oz/25g flaked almonds, toasted

1 onion, peeled and finely chopped

1 dessertspoon olive oil

a few saffron strands

4 cardamom pods, husked and the seeds separated

1 inch/2.5cm stick of cinnamon

black pepper

16 fl.oz/475ml water

Heat the oil and fry the onion until soft. Add the rice and stir around for 1 minute, then all remaining ingredients apart from the almonds and stir well. Bring to the boil, cover and simmer gently until the liquid has been absorbed. Remove from the heat and stir in three quarters of the almonds. Transfer to a warmed serving dish. Fork over and sprinkle the remaining almonds on top.

Bulgar, pepper and mushroom pilaff   (Serves 4)

8oz/225g bulgar wheat

8oz/225g red pepper

8oz/225g mushrooms, wiped and chopped

1 onion, peeled and minced

1 red chilli

2 garlic cloves, crushed

2 tablespoons olive oil

2 tablespoons finely chopped fresh parsley

1 teaspoon paprika

black pepper

16 fl.oz/475ml water

chopped walnuts

Grind the red pepper and chilli to a purée, then put into a pan with the onion, garlic and olive oil. Stir well and cook for 10 minutes, stirring occasionally. Add the remaining ingredients, except the walnuts, and combine well. Bring to the boil, cover and simmer gently for about 20 minutes until the liquid has been absorbed. Put into a warmed serving dish and garnish with chopped walnuts.

Rice with spinach   (Serves 4)

1lb/450g fresh spinach, finely shredded

8oz/225g long grain rice

1 onion, peeled and finely chopped

1 garlic clove, crushed

1 tablespoon olive oil

¼ teaspoon ground allspice

black pepper

20 fl.oz/600ml water

Heat the oil in a large pan and fry the onion and garlic until soft. Add the rice and fry for 1 minute more, then add the spinach and stir around until it wilts. Mix in the water and ground allspice and season with black pepper. Bring to the boil, cover and simmer gently until the liquid has been absorbed and the rice is done.

Wheat berry and green vegetable pilaff   (Serves 4/6)

8oz/225g wheat berries

4oz/100g courgette, chopped

4oz/100g green pepper, chopped

4oz/100g shelled peas

2 medium gherkins, finely chopped

1 onion, peeled and finely chopped

2 garlic cloves, crushed

1 dessertspoon olive oil

2 teaspoons cumin seed

2 teaspoons dried parsley

1 teaspoon dried mint

black pepper

20 fl.oz/600ml water

fresh mint leaves

Soak the wheat berries in boiling water for 2 hours. Drain and put them in a pan with fresh water, bring to the boil, cover and simmer for 45 minutes, then drain again.

In a large pan heat the oil and gently fry the onion and garlic until softened. Add the cumin seed and stir around for 30 seconds. Now add the wheat berries, parsley, dried mint and water, stir well and bring to the boil. Cover and simmer briskly for 10 minutes, then add the courgette, green pepper, peas and gherkins and season with black pepper. Mix well and continue simmering for about 20 minutes, until the liquid has been absorbed and the vegetables are tender. Spoon into a warmed serving dish and garnish with fresh mint leaves.

Brown rice with lentils   (Serves 4)

4oz/100g long grain brown rice

4oz/100g brown lentils

1 onion, peeled and finely chopped

2oz/50g sultanas

1 teaspoon coriander seed, crushed

1 teaspoon ground cumin

¼ teaspoon ground cardamom

1 dessertspoon olive oil

black pepper

18 fl.oz/550ml vegetable stock or water

chopped walnuts

Soak the lentils in water for 1 hour, drain and rinse and bring to the boil in fresh water. Cover and simmer briskly for 30 minutes, then drain.

Heat the oil and soften the onion. Add the rice and spices and stir around for

1 minute. Now add the lentils, sultanas and stock and combine well. Bring to the boil, cover and simmer gently until the liquid has been absorbed and the rice and lentils are cooked. Transfer to a warmed serving dish and garnish with chopped walnuts.

Garlic rice with potato topping   (Serves 4)

12oz/350g potato, peeled and sliced

6oz/175g basmati rice

2 garlic cloves, crushed

1 dessertspoon vegan margarine

15 fl.oz/475ml water

½ teaspoon turmeric

black pepper

finely sliced spring onions

finely chopped fresh coriander

Boil the potato slices for 3 minutes, then drain. Fry the garlic in the margarine in a large saucepan. Add the potato slices and stir around for 2 minutes. Cover the base of the pan with the slices. Mix the turmeric with the rice and add to the pan, spreading it evenly over the potato slices. Season with black pepper and slowly add the water. Bring to the boil, cover and simmer gently for about 25 minutes until all of the liquid has been absorbed. Carefully invert the pan onto a serving plate so that the potatoes are on top of the rice. Sprinkle with spring onions and fresh coriander before serving.

Tomato rice with mushrooms and broad beans

(Serves 4)

8oz/225g long grain rice

8oz/225g tomato, skinned and chopped

8oz/225g mushrooms, wiped and chopped

8oz/225g shelled broad beans

1 onion, peeled and finely chopped

2 garlic cloves, crushed

2 tablespoons finely chopped fresh coriander

1 tablespoon tomato purée

1 dessertspoon olive oil

1 rounded teaspoon cumin seed

1 teaspoon ground coriander

black pepper

16 fl.oz/475ml water

1 tomato, cut into wedges

chopped black olives

Blanch the broad beans in boiling water, drain and rinse under cold running water. Slip the skins from the beans and discard. Fry the onion and garlic in the oil in a large pan until soft. Add the rice, mushrooms, cumin seed and ground coriander and stir around for 1 minute. Dissolve the tomato purée in the water and add to the pan together with the broad beans, chopped tomato and fresh coriander. Season with black pepper and stir well. Bring to the boil, cover and simmer gently until the liquid has been absorbed and the rice is done. Put in a warmed serving dish and garnish with the tomato wedges and chopped olives.

Minted rice with noodles and peas   (Serves 4)

4oz/100g long grain rice

4oz/100g noodles, broken

4oz/100g shelled peas

1 onion, peeled and finely chopped

1 garlic clove, crushed

1 dessertspoon olive oil

2 rounded teaspoons dried mint, crumbled

black pepper

20 fl.oz/600ml water

fresh mint leaves

Fry the onion and garlic in the oil until softened. Add the rice and stir around for 30 seconds, then add the remaining ingredients apart from the fresh mint. Stir well and bring to the boil. Cover and simmer gently until the liquid has been absorbed and the rice and noodles are cooked. Spoon into a warmed serving dish and garnish with fresh mint leaves.

Orange and sultana rice   (Serves 4)

8oz/225g long grain rice

1 orange

2oz/50g sultanas

1 onion, peeled and finely chopped

1 tablespoon olive oil

1 teaspoon coriander seed, crushed

¼ teaspoon turmeric

black pepper

12 fl.oz/350ml water

6 fl.oz/175ml fresh orange juice

Grate the zest from the orange, then remove the pith and cut the orange into slices for garnish.

Gently fry the onion in the oil until soft. Add the rice and orange zest and fry for 1 minute more. Stir in the orange juice, water, sultanas, coriander and turmeric, season with black pepper and bring to the boil. Cover and simmer gently until the liquid has been absorbed and the rice is tender. Transfer to a warmed serving bowl and fork over. Garnish with the orange slices before serving.

Fruity vegetable pilaff   (Serves 4/6)

8oz/225g brown basmati rice

8oz/225g carrot, scraped and finely chopped

4oz/100g red pepper, chopped

4oz/100g shelled peas

2oz/50g dried apricots, finely chopped

2oz/50g dried dates, finely chopped

1oz/25g sultanas

1oz/25g mixed nuts, finely chopped

1 onion, peeled and finely chopped

2 garlic cloves, crushed

1 tablespoon olive oil

2 inch/5cm stick of cinnamon

6 cloves

1 teaspoon coriander seed, crushed

1 teaspoon cumin seed

½ teaspoon turmeric

black pepper

30 fl.oz/900ml water

Heat the oil in a large pan and gently soften the onion and garlic. Add the rice, cinnamon, cloves, coriander and cumin seed and turmeric and stir around for 1 minute. Add the remaining ingredients, except the nuts, and mix well. Bring to the boil, cover and simmer gently until the liquid has been absorbed and the rice and vegetables are tender. Stir in three quarters of the nuts, spoon the pilaff into a warmed serving dish and garnish with the remaining nuts.

Spiced brown rice with okra   (Serves 4)

1lb/450g okra, topped, tailed and cut into ½ inch/1cm diagonal slices

8oz/225g long grain brown rice

1 onion, peeled and finely chopped

2 garlic cloves, crushed

1 tablespoon olive oil

26 fl.oz/775ml water

2 inch/5cm stick of cinnamon, crumbled

6 cardamoms, husked and the seeds separated

1 rounded teaspoon cumin seed

1 rounded teaspoon ground coriander

½ teaspoon turmeric

black pepper

chopped fresh coriander leaves

Fry the onion and garlic in the oil until softened. Add the rice and spices and stir around for 1 minute, then stir in the okra and water and bring to the boil. Cover and simmer gently until the liquid has been absorbed and the rice and okra are done. Serve in a warmed dish garnished with chopped coriander.

SAUCES AND DRESSINGS

Savoury yoghurt-based dressings are common throughout the region and can give an instant Middle Eastern flavour to simple salads or plainly cooked vegetables. The garlic and herb dressing is a Lebanese speciality, which can be used equally well with green, rice, lentil or vegetable salads. Bowls of sauces and dressings are also served as part of a mezze for spooning over little savouries.

Tomato sauce   (Serves 4)

12oz/350g fresh ripe tomatoes, skinned and finely chopped

4 spring onions, trimmed and finely chopped

1 garlic clove, crushed

1 dessertspoon olive oil

1 dessertspoon tamarind purée

1 teaspoon lemon juice

½ teaspoon ground cumin

¼ teaspoon cayenne pepper

Fry the spring onions and garlic in the oil, then add the remaining ingredients. Stir well and bring to the boil. Cover and simmer, stirring occasionally, for 10 minutes. Mash the tomatoes with the back of a spoon and serve the sauce either hot or cold.

Red pepper and chilli sauce   (Serves 4)

12oz/350g red pepper, ground

1 red chilli, ground

2 garlic cloves, crushed

2 tablespoons olive oil

1 dessertspoon red wine vinegar

black pepper

2 rounded tablespoons plain soya yoghurt

Put the red pepper, chilli, garlic, oil and vinegar in a small saucepan. Season with black pepper and stir well, then bring to the boil, cover and simmer for 10 minutes, stirring occasionally. Remove from the heat and stir in the yoghurt. Return to the heat and simmer for another minute or two while stirring. Serve hot.

Tahini sauce   (Serves 4)

2 rounded tablespoons light tahini

2 tablespoons water

2 dessertspoons lemon juice

1 garlic clove, crushed

black pepper

Mix the ingredients until well combined.

Pine kernel sauce   (Serves 4)

2oz/50g pine kernels, ground and toasted

2oz/50g French bread, diced

4 fl.oz/125ml soya milk

2 dessertspoons lemon juice

black pepper

2 fl.oz/50ml water

Soak the French bread in the soya milk for 20 minutes, then put in a blender together with any remaining liquid. Add the pine kernels, lemon juice and water and season with black pepper and blend until smooth. Serve cold or heat gently in a double boiler to serve hot.

Hazelnut sauce   (Serves 4)

As pine kernel sauce above, but replace the pine kernels with 2oz/50g ground and toasted hazelnuts.

Walnut and parsley dressing (Serves 4)

2oz/50g walnuts, grated

2 rounded tablespoons finely chopped fresh parsley

4 rounded tablespoons plain soya yoghurt

1 garlic clove, crushed

1 tablespoon lemon juice

1 tablespoon olive oil

1 tablespoon water

black pepper

Mix the ingredients well and chill before serving.

Tahini and yoghurt dressing (Serves 4)

2 rounded tablespoons light tahini

5 rounded tablespoons plain soya yoghurt

1 tablespoon lemon juice

1 garlic clove, crushed

1 rounded teaspoon parsley

black pepper

Combine all the ingredients and serve chilled.

Coriander, garlic and yoghurt dressing (Serves 4)

6 fl.oz/175ml plain soya yoghurt

4 rounded tablespoons finely chopped fresh coriander

2 garlic cloves, crushed

black pepper

Mix the ingredients together and refrigerate before serving.

Minted cucumber and yoghurt dressing   (Serves 4)

6 fl.oz/175ml plain soya yoghurt

4oz/100g cucumber, finely chopped

1 rounded teaspoon dried mint, crumbled

black pepper

Mix the ingredients and chill.

Garlic and herb dressing   (Serves 4)

4 heaped tablespoons finely chopped fresh herbs (a mixture of
    parsley, chives, oregano and thyme)

2 garlic cloves, chopped

2 medium gherkins, chopped

2 spring onions, trimmed and chopped

6 tablespoons olive oil

2 dessertspoons lemon juice

1 dessertspoon white wine vinegar

black pepper

Put all ingredients in a blender and blend until smooth.

VEGETABLES

All the vegetable dishes included here can be served as accompaniments to the main courses. Some also make ideal fillings for pitta bread, which can then be served with salad as a light meal. For quickly made vegetable dishes with a Middle Eastern flavour, simply steam some vegetables such as potatoes, green beans, cauliflower, broccoli, carrots or courgettes and serve topped with a sauce or dressing (pages 72-76).

Green lentils with spinach

(Serves 4)

8oz/225g fresh spinach, shredded

4oz/100g green lentils

1 onion, peeled and finely chopped

2 garlic cloves, crushed

1 dessertspoon olive oil

1 rounded teaspoon cumin seed

¼ teaspoon ground allspice

black pepper

plain soya yoghurt

Soak the lentils in boiling water for an hour, then drain and rinse and bring to the boil in fresh water. Cover and simmer for 30 minutes. Drain over a bowl and keep the cooking liquid.

Heat the oil in a large pan and fry the onion and garlic until soft. Add the spices and spinach and cook for 5 minutes, stirring occasionally. Pour the lentil liquid into a measuring jug and make up to 10 fl.oz/300ml, if necessary, with water. Add to the pan together with the lentils, stir well and bring to the boil. Cover and simmer for 15 minutes, then uncover and simmer for a further 5 minutes or so, stirring until the liquid has been absorbed. Transfer to a warmed serving dish and garnish with a swirl of yoghurt, or use as a filling for pitta bread.

Minted mashed potatoes

(Serves 4)

2lb/900g potatoes, peeled

3 tablespoons olive oil

2 rounded tablespoons plain soya yoghurt

1 rounded tablespoon dried mint, crumbled

1 tablespoon lemon juice

1 garlic clove, crushed

black pepper

fresh mint leaves

Cut the potatoes into even-sized chunks and cook them. Drain and dry off over a low heat. Mix the olive oil with the lemon juice, dried mint and garlic. Add to the potatoes together with the yoghurt and mash thoroughly, then spoon into a greased ovenproof dish. Cover and put in a preheated oven at 180°C/350°F/Gas mark 4 for about 15 minutes until heated through. Garnish with fresh mint leaves when serving.

Mixed beans with tomato sauce   (Serves 4)

8oz/225g green beans, topped, tailed and cut into 1/2 inch/1cm lengths

8oz/225g cooked mixed beans

chopped fresh coriander

sauce

8oz/225g ripe tomato, skinned and chopped

1 garlic clove, crushed

1 dessertspoon olive oil

1 dessertspoon tomato purée

1 tablespoon water

1 teaspoon lemon juice

1/2 teaspoon paprika

1/2 teaspoon cumin seed

black pepper

Heat the oil and fry the garlic. Add the tomato and cook until pulpy, then the remaining sauce ingredients and simmer, stirring occasionally, for 10 minutes. Meanwhile, steam the green beans until just tender. Add the cooked mixed beans to the sauce and simmer for 2 minutes. Remove from the heat and stir in the green beans. Spoon into a warmed dish and serve garnished with chopped coriander. This also makes an ideal filling for pitta bread.

Green vegetables with tomatoes   (Serves 6)

1lb/450g mixed green vegetables (e.g. okra, courgette, green
  pepper, broccoli)

1 onion, peeled and finely chopped

2 garlic cloves, crushed

1 green chilli, finely chopped

14oz/400g tin crushed tomatoes

1 tablespoon olive oil

2 tablespoons finely chopped fresh coriander

1 teaspoon coriander seed, crushed

¼ teaspoon paprika

black pepper

1 dessertspoon lemon juice

chopped fresh parsley

Gently fry the onion, garlic and chilli in the oil in a large pan until softened. Chop the vegetables into even-sized pieces and add to the pan together with the tomatoes, fresh and crushed coriander and paprika. Season with black pepper and stir well, then bring to the boil. Cover and simmer gently for about 25 minutes, stirring occasionally, until the vegetables are tender. Stir in the lemon juice, transfer to a warmed serving dish and garnish with parsley, or use as a pitta bread filling.

Saffron potatoes   (Serves 4)

2lb/900g potatoes, peeled and cut into ¼ inch/5mm slices

8 fl.oz/225ml soya milk, warmed

1 rounded dessertspoon vegan margarine

a few strands of saffron

black pepper

finely chopped spring onions

Boil the potatoes for 3 minutes, then drain. Melt the margarine in a large pan and add the potato slices. Stir around for 1 minute, until the potatoes are coated in margarine. Dissolve the saffron in the soya milk and add, season with black pepper and bring to the boil. Simmer for 3 minutes, then put into a greased baking dish. Cover tightly and bake in a preheated oven at 180°C/350°F/Gas mark 4 for about 30 minutes until done. Garnish with chopped spring onions and serve.

Sesame carrots with raisins (Serves 4)

1lb/450g carrots, peeled and grated

1oz/25g raisins

1 tablespoon olive oil

8 fl.oz/225ml water

2 fl.oz/50ml fresh orange juice

1 rounded tablespoon light tahini

½ teaspoon paprika

black pepper

toasted sesame seeds

Fry the carrots in the oil for 3 minutes. Add the raisins, water, orange juice and paprika and season with black pepper, stir well and bring to the boil. Cover and simmer for about 15 minutes, stirring occasionally, until the liquid has been absorbed and the carrot is cooked. Add the tahini and stir until dissolved and well combined. Transfer to a warmed serving dish and sprinkle with toasted sesame seeds.

Broccoli with mushrooms and almonds (Serves 4)

1lb/450g broccoli, chopped

4oz/100g mushrooms, wiped and finely chopped

2 garlic cloves, crushed

2oz/50g flaked almonds, toasted

1 dessertspoon olive oil

1 rounded teaspoon ground cumin

1 rounded teaspoon dried parsley

black pepper

12 fl.oz/350ml water

8 fl.oz/225ml soya milk

1 rounded dessertspoon cornflour

Fry the mushrooms and garlic in the oil until the juices begin to run. Add the cumin and stir around for 30 seconds, then the broccoli, parsley and water. Season with black pepper, stir well and bring to the boil. Cover and simmer for about 10 minutes until the broccoli is just tender. Keep a tablespoonful of almonds for garnish, finely crumble the rest and add to the pan. Dissolve the cornflour in the soya milk and add, then stir well and bring to the boil. Continue stirring for a minute or two until the sauce thickens. Serve garnished with the remaining almonds. Can also be used as a filling for pitta bread.

Aubergine with borlotti beans   (Serves 4)

12oz/350g aubergine, diced

6oz/175g ripe tomato, skinned and chopped

4oz/100g cooked borlotti beans

1 onion, peeled and finely chopped

1 garlic clove, crushed

2 tablespoons olive oil

2 tablespoons water

1 dessertspoon tomato purée

1 teaspoon dried basil

1 teaspoon dried thyme

¼ teaspoon cayenne pepper

black pepper

1 bay leaf

1 dessertspoon lemon juice

fresh basil leaves

Fry the aubergine, onion and garlic in the oil for 10 minutes, stirring occasionally. Add the tomato, water, tomato purée, dried basil, thyme, cayenne pepper and bay leaf. Season with black pepper and stir well. Bring to the boil, cover and simmer for 10-15 minutes until the aubergine is tender, stirring frequently to prevent sticking. Add the beans and lemon juice and continue simmering for a minute or two. Spoon into a warmed serving dish and garnish with fresh basil leaves or use as a filling for pitta bread.

Potato latkes   (Makes 12)

2lb/900g potatoes, peeled

1 onion, peeled and minced

1 garlic clove, crushed

½ teaspoon dried dill

½ teaspoon dried parsley

black pepper

olive oil

Cut the potatoes into large even-sized chunks and boil for 5 minutes. Drain and allow to cool, then grate them into a mixing bowl. Add the onion, garlic, dill and parsley, season with black pepper and mix very well. Take rounded tablespoonfuls of the mixture and fry them for a few minutes on each side in hot oil until golden. Drain on kitchen paper.

Cabbage with garlic and thyme dressing   (Serves 4)

12oz/350g green cabbage leaves

dressing

1 tablespoon olive oil

2 tablespoons finely chopped fresh thyme

1 garlic clove, crushed

1 dessertspoon lemon juice

black pepper

Cut the thick stalks from the cabbage leaves, finely shred the leaves and steam them until tender. Mix the dressing ingredients together and add to the cooked cabbage. Toss well before serving.

Stuffed baked potatoes   (Serves 4)

4 potatoes, each approx. 8oz/225g

olive oil

filling

8oz/225g mushrooms, wiped and finely chopped

1oz/25g sultanas, chopped

1oz/25g walnuts, finely chopped

2 garlic cloves, crushed

2 tablespoons olive oil

1 teaspoon ground cumin

black pepper

fresh parsley sprigs

Wash the potatoes and slit them lengthwise with a sharp knife. Brush them all over with olive oil and put them on a baking tray. Cover with foil and bake in a preheated oven at 200°C/400°F/Gas mark 6 for about 1 hour until done.

Meanwhile, make the filling. Fry the mushrooms and garlic in the oil until the juices run from the mushrooms. Add the cumin and stir around for 30 seconds, then remove from the heat and add the sultanas and half of the walnuts. Season with black pepper and mix well. Scoop out the centres of the cooked potatoes, leaving the skins intact. Mash the scooped out potato and add to the filling. Combine well and spoon the filling into the potato shells. Sprinkle the remaining walnuts on top and return the stuffed potatoes to the oven, uncovered, for 15 minutes. Garnish with fresh parsley sprigs when serving.

SALADS

With so many inspiring ingredients to choose from, Middle Eastern cooks regularly prepare a wide variety of colourful, appetising and nutritious salads. All types of grains, beans and lentils are combined with fruits and vegetables and subtly flavoured with fresh and dried herbs and spices. Stale bread is never wasted and this is often toasted, cut into squares and added to salads just before serving so that it remains crisp. A salad may be served with bread as a light meal or used as a filling for pitta bread. Bowls of salad are also often served with main courses or as part of a mezze. Some traditional dishes such as fattoush and tabbouleh have become firm favourites in many other parts of the world.

Fruity pepper and bulgar salad   (Serves 6)

8oz/225g mixed peppers, finely chopped

4oz/100g bulgar wheat

2oz/50g sultanas

4 fresh apricots, stoned and finely chopped

8 black grapes, quartered

8 fl.oz/225ml fresh orange juice

1 dessertspoon olive oil

1 dessertspoon lemon juice

1 teaspoon coriander seeds, crushed

black pepper

chopped fresh parsley

Bring the orange juice to the boil, remove from the heat and add the bulgar wheat. Cover and leave for 30 minutes. Put in a sieve and press out any excess liquid with the back of a spoon, then keep in the fridge in a covered bowl until cold. When cold add all remaining ingredients apart from the parsley and mix well. Serve garnished with chopped parsley.

Mixed chopped salad   (Serves 4)

4oz/100g tomato

4oz/100g green pepper

4oz/100g red pepper

4oz/100g cucumber

4 spring onions, trimmed and sliced

1 garlic clove, crushed

½ green chilli, crushed

1 teaspoon dried parsley

1 teaspoon dried mint

1 teaspoon lemon juice

1 dessertspoon olive oil

black pepper

shredded lettuce leaves

chopped fresh coriander leaves

Finely chop the tomato, green and red peppers and cucumber and put them in a mixing bowl with the spring onions. Mix the garlic, chilli, parsley, mint, lemon juice and olive oil together and add to the salad. Season with black pepper and combine thoroughly. Arrange some shredded lettuce leaves on a serving plate and pile the chopped salad on top. Garnish with chopped coriander.

Mushroom and bean salad   (Serves 4)

8oz/225g button mushrooms, wiped and sliced

8oz/225g mixed cooked beans

4 spring onions, trimmed and sliced

2 garlic cloves, crushed

½oz/15g fresh parsley, finely chopped

1 tablespoon olive oil

1 dessertspoon lemon juice

black pepper

shredded lettuce leaves

Fry the mushrooms and garlic in the oil for a couple of minutes until the juices just begin to run from the mushrooms. Transfer to a mixing bowl, cover and refrigerate for a few hours until cold. Add the beans, spring onions, parsley and lemon juice. Season with black pepper and mix well. Spread some shredded lettuce on a serving plate and pile the salad on top.

Broad bean tabbouleh   (Serves 4/6)

12oz/350g shelled broad beans

4oz/100g bulgar wheat

8 fl.oz/225ml boiling water

4 spring onions, trimmed and finely sliced

4 green olives, finely chopped

4 rounded tablespoons finely chopped fresh mint

black pepper

1 dessertspoon olive oil

1 dessertspoon white wine vinegar

2 dessertspoons lemon juice

shredded crisp lettuce leaves

cucumber slices, halved

fresh mint leaves

Soak the bulgar in the boiling water for 30 minutes. Spoon into a sieve and press out any excess liquid with the back of a spoon. Put the bulgar in a mixing bowl and add the spring onions, olives and chopped mint. Cook the broad beans until tender, rinse them under cold running water and slip them from their skins. Add the beans to the bulgar. Mix the olive oil with the vinegar and lemon juice and add to the salad, season with black pepper and mix well. Arrange some shredded lettuce on a serving plate and pile the salad on top. Garnish with the cucumber slices and mint leaves.

Minted potato salad   (Serves 4)

1½lb/675g new potatoes, scraped

fresh mint leaves

dressing

1 tablespoon olive oil

1 tablespoon white wine vinegar

1 tablespoon lemon juice

1 dessertspoon dried mint, crumbled

black pepper

Cook the potatoes, drain and dice. Mix the dressing ingredients together. Put the potatoes into a mixing bowl, add the dressing and toss until the potatoes are coated. Serve warm or cold garnished with fresh mint leaves.

Cauliflower with tomato dressing   (Serves 4)

12oz/350g cauliflower, cut into tiny florets

6oz/175g ripe tomato, skinned and chopped

4 spring onions, trimmed and finely sliced

1 garlic clove, crushed

1 tablespoon olive oil

1 tablespoon red wine vinegar

2 tablespoons finely chopped fresh parsley

¼ teaspoon cayenne pepper

black pepper

Heat the oil and gently fry the garlic. Add the tomato and cook for a couple of minutes until softened. Remove from the heat and add the vinegar, parsley and cayenne pepper. Season with black pepper and mix well. Steam the cauliflower until tender, then rinse under cold running water, drain and put in a mixing bowl with half of the sliced onions. Add the tomato dressing and toss well. Transfer to a serving dish and garnish with the remaining onions. Cover and chill before serving.

Chickpea and pepper salad   (Serves 4)

8oz/225g cooked chickpeas

4oz/100g red pepper

4oz/100g green pepper, finely chopped

4 spring onions, trimmed and sliced

1 garlic clove, crushed

1 dessertspoon olive oil

1 teaspoon lemon juice

¼ teaspoon cayenne pepper

black pepper

shredded lettuce leaves

chopped fresh coriander leaves

Grind the red pepper to a paste and put in a mixing bowl with the garlic, oil, lemon juice and cayenne pepper. Season with black pepper and mix well. Add the chickpeas, green pepper and spring onions and toss thoroughly. Spread some shredded lettuce on a serving plate, pile the salad on top and garnish with chopped coriander.

Aubergine and bulgar salad   (Serves 4)

4oz/100g aubergine, finely chopped

4oz/100g bulgar wheat

4oz/100g ripe tomato, skinned and finely chopped

1 onion, peeled and finely chopped

1 garlic clove, crushed

2 tablespoons olive oil

8 fl.oz/225ml boiling water

1 tablespoon finely chopped fresh coriander leaves

1 teaspoon lemon juice

1 teaspoon red wine vinegar

1 teaspoon tamarind purée

1 teaspoon ground cumin

¼ teaspoon cayenne pepper

black pepper

shredded lettuce leaves

Fry the aubergine, onion and garlic in the oil for 20 minutes until soft. Remove from the heat and add the bulgar, cumin, cayenne pepper and water. Season with black pepper and stir well. Cover and allow to stand for 30 minutes. Combine the tomato with the lemon juice, vinegar and tamarind and add to the salad together with the coriander. Mix very well, then cover and chill for a few hours. Arrange some shredded lettuce on a serving plate. Fork through the salad and pile it on top of the lettuce.

Courgette and green lentil salad   (Serves 4)

8oz/225g courgette, chopped

4oz/100g green lentils

1 garlic clove, crushed

4 spring onions, trimmed and finely sliced

1 dessertspoon lemon juice

1 dessertspoon olive oil

1 teaspoon dried mint

1 teaspoon dried thyme

black pepper

fresh mint leaves

Soak the lentils in boiling water for an hour, drain and rinse and put in a fresh pan of water. Bring to the boil, cover and simmer for 30 minutes until done. Drain and rinse and place in a mixing bowl with the garlic, spring onions, mint and thyme. Lightly steam the courgette for a couple of minutes to soften, then rinse under cold running water to refresh. Drain well and add to the salad. Combine the lemon juice with the olive oil and spoon over the salad. Season with black pepper and mix well. Spoon into a serving bowl and garnish with fresh mint.

Herby wheat salad   (Serves 4)

4oz/100g wheat berries

4oz/100g shelled broad beans

4oz/100g shelled peas

3 rounded tablespoons finely chopped mixed fresh herbs (e.g. parsley, thyme, mint, oregano)

3 spring onions, trimmed and finely chopped

2oz/50g green pepper

1 garlic clove

1 gherkin

1 dessertspoon olive oil

1 teaspoon lemon juice

black pepper

1 tomato, cut into wedges

Put the wheat berries in a bowl and cover with boiling water. Leave to soak for 2 hours, then drain and rinse and bring to the boil in fresh water. Cover and simmer briskly for an hour, topping up with more boiling water when necessary. Drain and rinse under cold running water, drain well and put in a mixing bowl. Cook the broad beans until tender, rinse under cold water. Slip the beans from their skins and add to the wheat. Cook the peas until tender, rinse under cold water and add to the salad together with the chopped herbs and spring onions. Blend the green pepper with the gherkin, garlic, oil and lemon juice until smooth. Spoon this dressing over the salad and season with black pepper. Toss thoroughly and transfer the salad to a serving bowl. Arrange the tomato wedges around the edge of the bowl.

Brown lentil and pitta salad   (Serves 4)

4oz/100g brown lentils

1 small onion, peeled and minced

1 garlic clove, crushed

1 tablespoon olive oil

1 inch/2.5cm stick of cinnamon

½ teaspoon cumin seed

½ teaspoon ground coriander

1 dessertspoon lemon juice

black pepper

1 rounded tablespoon plain soya yoghurt

1 pitta bread

chopped fresh coriander leaves

Soak the lentils in boiling water for an hour, then drain and put in a pan of fresh water with the cinnamon. Bring to the boil, cover and simmer for about 30 minutes until done. Drain and discard the cinnamon. Heat the oil and gently fry the onion and garlic to soften. Add the cumin seed and ground coriander and fry for 30 seconds. Remove from the heat and add the lentils and lemon juice. Season with black pepper and stir well. Cover and refrigerate until cold.

Slice the pitta bread in half, toast it and cut it into small squares. Add first the yoghurt and then the toasted pitta squares to the cold lentil salad and garnish with chopped coriander.

Arabian bean salad   (Serves 4)

8oz/225g green beans, topped, tailed and cut into ¹/₂ inch/1cm
    lengths

8oz/225g mixed cooked beans

8oz/225g ripe tomato, skinned and finely chopped

4 spring onions, trimmed and finely sliced

1 garlic clove, crushed

2 tablespoons finely chopped fresh parsley

1 dessertspoon olive oil

1 dessertspoon lemon juice

black pepper

chopped black olives

Steam the green beans until just tender and rinse them under cold running water. Drain and put in a bowl with the mixed beans, spring onions, garlic and parsley. Combine the olive oil and lemon juice with the tomato and add. Season with black pepper and mix well. Spoon into a serving bowl and garnish with chopped olives.

Cucumber and green pea salad   (Serves 4)

8oz/225g cucumber, diced

8oz/225g shelled peas

4 spring onions, trimmed and finely sliced

8 green olives, chopped

2 medium gherkins, chopped

1 garlic clove, crushed

1 small green chilli, finely chopped

1 dessertspoon olive oil

1 dessertspoon lemon juice

1 teaspoon dried mint, crumbled

black pepper

fresh mint leaves

Blanch the peas until tender, then drain and refresh under cold running water. Drain and put in a mixing bowl with the cucumber, spring onions, olives, gherkins, garlic, chilli and dried mint. Season with black pepper and stir well. Mix the olive oil with the lemon juice and add to the salad. Toss thoroughly, transfer the salad to a serving bowl and garnish it with fresh mint leaves.

Fattoush   (Serves 4)

1 little gem lettuce, chopped

4oz/100g cucumber, chopped

4oz/100g green pepper, chopped

8 cherry tomatoes, quartered

6 spring onions, trimmed and chopped

2 tablespoons fresh mint leaves

2 tablespoons fresh parsley leaves

a few purslane leaves (optional)

1 pitta bread

1 garlic clove, crushed

2 dessertspoons olive oil

2 dessertspoons lemon juice

black pepper

Stir the lettuce, cucumber, green pepper, tomatoes, onions, mint, parsley and purslane leaves together in a large bowl. Mix the garlic with the olive oil and lemon juice and add to the salad, season with black pepper and toss. Split the pitta bread in half and toast it, cut it into squares and add these to the salad. Toss well.

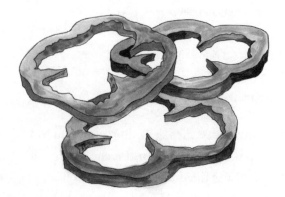

Barley and vegetable salad   (Serves 4)

4oz/100g pot barley

2oz/50g green beans, topped, tailed and cut into $1/2$ inch/1cm
    lengths

2oz/50g shelled peas

2oz/50g broccoli, chopped

2oz/50g cauliflower, chopped

4 spring onions, trimmed and finely sliced

6 green olives, chopped

1 dessertspoon olive oil

1 dessertspoon white wine vinegar

1 dessertspoon lemon juice

$1/2$ teaspoon dried dill

$1/2$ teaspoon dried mint

$1/8$ teaspoon cayenne pepper

black pepper

fresh mint leaves

Soak the barley in boiling water for 1 hour, then drain and place in a fresh pan of water. Bring to the boil, cover and simmer for about an hour until done. Drain and rinse under cold running water. Drain well and put in a mixing bowl. Steam the vegetables until just tender, then rinse under cold water to refresh. Drain and add to the barley together with the spring onions and olives. Mix the olive oil with the vinegar, lemon juice, dill, mint and cayenne pepper. Season with black pepper and combine well. Spoon the dressing over the salad and toss. Transfer to a serving bowl, cover and chill for a couple of hours. Garnish with fresh mint leaves when serving.

BREADS

Bread is highly revered in all Middle Eastern countries and it is in this region that flatbreads are believed to have originated around 9,000 years ago. Some form of bread is eaten at every meal, either to mop up soups, stews and casseroles or, in the case of pitta bread, split open and filled with savoury mixtures. Bread is never wasted and stale bread is used in various ways in other dishes.

Lebanese herb bread   (Serves 4)

8oz/225g plain flour
½ sachet easy-blend yeast
pinch of salt
1 tablespoon dried thyme
1 tablespoon dried oregano
2 tablespoons olive oil
approx. 4 fl.oz/125ml warm water
   topping
1 tablespoon olive oil
1 dessertspoon sesame seeds
1 teaspoon dried thyme
1 teaspoon dried oregano

Mix the flour, yeast, salt, thyme and oregano, then add the olive oil and combine well. Gradually add the water until a soft dough forms. Turn out onto a floured board and knead thoroughly. Divide the dough into 4 equal pieces and shape each piece into a ball, then flatten by hand or roll into a circle of about 4½ inches/11.5cm. Transfer the circles to a greased baking sheet, cover with a piece of oiled cling film and leave in a warm place for 1 hour to rise. Mix the topping ingredients together and spread evenly over the top of the dough. Bake in a preheated oven at 200°C/400°F/Gas mark 6 for about 12 minutes until golden brown. Serve warm.

Pitta bread   (Makes 6/12)

8oz/225g plain flour
½ teaspoon salt
½ sachet easy-blend yeast
approx. 5 fl.oz/150ml warm water
olive oil

Sift the flour, salt and yeast into a mixing bowl and gradually add the water until a soft dough forms. Knead well for 5 minutes, then return the dough to the bowl. Cover and leave in a warm place for an hour until risen. Turn out onto a floured board and knead again. Divide the dough into 6, 8 or 12 equal pieces, depending on the size of pittas required. Roll each piece into a ball, then roll them out into a thin oval shape. Put the ovals on baking sheets, cover and leave in a warm place for 30 minutes. Lightly grease a non-stick frying pan with olive oil and heat until hot. Fry each pitta bread for about 1 minute on each side over a moderate heat, until browned and puffed up. Serve warm.

Turkish cornbread   (Serves 8)

6oz/175g fine cornmeal
6oz/175g self raising flour
4 tablespoons olive oil
½ teaspoon salt
8 fl.oz/225ml plain soya yoghurt
5 fl.oz/150ml soya milk

Combine the cornmeal with the flour and salt in a large bowl, then add the olive oil and mix well. Gradually add the yoghurt and soya milk and stir thoroughly until a soft dropping consistency is achieved. Pour the dough into a lined and greased 8 inch/20cm diameter baking tin and level the top. Bake in a preheated oven at 190°C/375°F/Gas mark 5 for 30-35 minutes until golden brown. Carefully turn out of the tin, cut into wedges and serve warm.

Persian naan   (Serves 4)

8oz/225g plain flour

1 tablespoon olive oil

1 rounded teaspoon easy-blend yeast

½ teaspoon salt

approx. 5 fl.oz/150ml warm water

extra olive oil

sesame seeds

Mix the flour with the salt and yeast in a mixing bowl. Add the tablespoonful of olive oil and stir well. Gradually add the water until a soft dough is formed. Knead well and return to the bowl, cover and leave to rise in a warm place for 1 hour. Knead the dough again and put it on a greased baking sheet. Form it into a large pear shape of about ½ inch/1cm thick. Cover and leave in a warm place for 30 minutes. Brush the top with oil, sprinkle it with sesame seeds and bake in a preheated oven at 200°C/400°F/Gas mark 6 for about 10 minutes until golden. Serve warm.

Minted flat bread   (Makes 8)

12oz/350g plain flour

½ sachet easy-blend yeast

1 rounded tablespoon dried mint, crumbled

1 tablespoon olive oil

½ teaspoon salt

approx. 7½ fl.oz/212ml warm water

extra olive oil

Put the flour, yeast, mint and salt in a bowl and mix together. Add the tablespoonful of oil and combine well. Gradually add the water to form a soft dough. Knead thoroughly, return it to the bowl, cover and leave for 1 hour in a warm place until risen. Knead the dough again and divide it into 8 equal pieces. Roll each piece into a ball, then roll it out into a circle measuring 5 inches/13cm in diameter. Place the circles on greased baking sheets and cover with oiled cling film. Leave in a warm place for 30 minutes to rise. Brush the tops with olive oil and bake in a preheated oven at 200°C/400°F/Gas mark 6 for about 10 minutes until browned. Serve warm.

Sun-dried tomato and olive bread   (Makes 4)

8oz/225g plain flour

½ sachet easy-blend yeast

½ teaspoon salt

1oz/25g sun-dried tomato, finely chopped

2 tablespoons olive oil

1 dessertspoon dried basil

approx. 4 fl.oz/125ml warm water

12 black olives, halved

extra olive oil

Soak the tomato in the 2 tablespoonfuls of olive oil overnight. Put the flour, yeast, salt and basil in a bowl, add the soaked tomato and remaining oil and mix well. Gradually add the warm water until a soft dough forms. Knead well and divide into 4 equal pieces. Roll each piece of dough into a ball, then shape it into a 4 inch/10cm circle. Put the circles on a greased baking sheet, cover and allow to rise for 1 hour in a warm place. Brush the circles with olive oil and press 6 olive halves in the top of each one. Bake in a preheated oven at 200°C/400°F/Gas mark 6 for about 15 minutes until golden brown. Serve warm.

DESSERTS

Citrus fruits, dates and figs are probably the best known fruits to be exported from the Middle East, but other fruits such as mangoes, bananas, papayas, melons, grapes, apples, apricots and various soft fruits are also widely grown in the fertile valleys of Lebanon, Syria, Iraq, Israel, Jordan, Yemen and Oman. Fruit salads made from a selection of these fruits and served in a light sugar syrup or in fruit juice flavoured with rose flower water also makes an authentic Middle Eastern dessert.

Bride's fingers   (Makes 12)

10z/300g packet filo pastry

2oz/50g vegan margarine, melted

sesame seeds

filling

4oz/100g walnuts, grated

2oz/50g ground rice

2oz/50g dried apricots, finely chopped

5 fl.oz/150ml water

1 dessertspoon rose water

soya milk

½ teaspoon ground cinnamon

¼ teaspoon ground coriander

syrup

1oz/25g soft brown sugar

4 fl.oz.125ml water

1 teaspoon lemon juice

Soak the apricots in the water for 2 hours, then strain the liquid into a measuring jug and add the rose water. Make up to 8 fl.oz/225ml with soya milk and pour the liquid into a saucepan. Add the ground rice, cinnamon and coriander, stir well and bring to the boil while stirring. Simmer for about 1 minute until thick. Remove from the heat and add the apricots and walnuts. Mix thoroughly and allow to cool.

Put the filo sheets on a flat surface. Cut the stack into 3 equal rectangles and each of these in half, to measure about 10 x 5 inches/25 x 13cm. Brush 12 of the filo rectangles with melted margarine and place another sheet on top of each one. Put a rounded tablespoonful of filling on one end of each rectangle. Fold the two long edges over and roll up from the short edge to enclose the filling and make a finger shape. Transfer the fingers to a greased baking dish and brush with melted margarine. Sprinkle with sesame seeds and bake in a preheated oven at 180°C/350°F/Gas mark 4 for about 25 minutes until golden.

Meanwhile make the syrup. Put the sugar, water and lemon juice in a small pan and bring to the boil. Simmer, whilst stirring occasionally, for 10-15 minutes until the mixture reduces and becomes syrupy. Pour the hot syrup over the hot 'fingers' in the dish and allow to cool before serving.

Apricot and hazelnut yoghurt   (Serves 4)

8oz/225g dried apricots, finely chopped

16 fl.oz/475ml water

1oz/25g hazelnuts, ground and lightly toasted

10 fl.oz/300ml plain soya yoghurt

toasted flaked hazelnuts

Put the apricots and water in a saucepan, cover and leave to soak for 1 hour. Bring to the boil, cover and simmer for 15 minutes. Remove from the heat and mash until smooth, then add the ground hazelnuts and mix well. Cover and refrigerate until cold. When cold, add the yoghurt and combine thoroughly. Spoon into 4 serving bowls and sprinkle with flaked hazelnuts.

Mango milk pudding   (Serves 4)

14oz/400g tin mango slices in syrup

8 fl.oz./225ml soya milk

½ oz/15g cornflour

1 dessertspoon orange flower water

Keep 8 thin slices of mango for garnish and put the rest with the syrup in a blender with the orange flower water. Mix the cornflour with the soya milk until smooth and add. Blend until smooth, then transfer to a double boiler and stir while bringing to the boil. Continue stirring until the mixture thickens. Pour the sauce into 4 glasses, cover and chill for a few hours until set. Garnish with the remaining mango slices and serve with sesame biscuits (see page 117).

Dried fruit salad   (Serves 6)

1lb/450g mixed dried fruit (e.g. prunes, dates, figs, apples, pears, peaches, apricots)

2oz/50g sultanas

20 fl.oz.600ml water

1 tablespoon orange flower water

2 inch/5cm stick of cinnamon, broken in half

6 cloves

Put all the ingredients in a saucepan and stir well. Bring to the boil, cover and simmer for 5 minutes. Transfer to a lidded container and keep in the fridge for at least 12 hours. Then remove the spices and serve the fruit with yoghurt.

Banana custard   (Serves 4)

2 bananas (each approx. 5oz/150g)

12 fl.oz/350ml soya milk

1 rounded tablespoon cornflour

1 rounded tablespoon soft brown sugar

ground cinnamon

Peel and chop one of the bananas and put it in a blender with the soya milk, cornflour and sugar. Blend until smooth, then pour into a double boiler and bring to the boil while stirring. Continue stirring until the custard thickens. Divide it between 4 glasses. Peel and slice the other banana and arrange the slices on top of the custard. Sprinkle with ground cinnamon and serve hot.

Carrot and cardamom pudding   (Serves 4)

1lb/450g carrots, scraped and grated

1oz/25g sultanas

10 fl.oz/300ml fresh orange juice

1oz/25g soft brown sugar

¼ teaspoon ground cardamom

1 dessertspoon vegan margarine

8 fl.oz/225ml soya milk

1 rounded dessertspoon cornflour

toasted flaked almonds

Put the carrots, sultanas, orange juice, sugar and cardamom in a saucepan and bring to the boil. Cover and simmer, stirring occasionally, for 25 minutes. Add the margarine and stir around until it melts. Dissolve the cornflour in the soya milk and add to the pan. Bring to the boil while stirring and continue stirring until the mixture thickens, then spoon it into 4 glasses. Cover and chill for a few hours and serve garnished with toasted flaked almonds.

Apricot and orange fruit salad   (Serves 4)

6oz/175g dried apricots, chopped

2 oranges

2oz/50g dates, chopped

10 black grapes, halved

8 fl.oz/225ml fresh orange juice

1 teaspoon orange flower water

chopped pistachios

Bring the apricots and orange juice to the boil, cover and simmer for 10 minutes. Put in a mixing bowl and allow to cool. Peel the oranges and discard all the pith, membranes and pips. Chop the segments and add to the apricots together with the dates, grapes and orange flower water. Mix well, then cover and chill. Serve garnished with chopped pistachios.

Pistachio and yoghurt ice   (Serves 4)

10 fl.oz/300ml plain soya yoghurt

2oz/50g pistachios, ground

1oz/25g sugar, ground

Mix the ingredients together until smooth. Spoon into a freezerproof container, cover and freeze for about 3 hours until just frozen. Keep at room temperature for an hour before serving if it becomes too solid.

Semolina and pine kernel pudding   (Serves 4)

2oz/50g semolina

1oz/25g pine kernels, toasted and grated

1oz/25g soft brown sugar

1 rounded dessertspoon vegan margarine

8 fl.oz/225ml soya milk

8 fl.oz/225ml water

¼ teaspoon ground cinnamon

toasted pine kernels

Gently heat the margarine until melted. Remove from the heat and add the semolina, grated pine kernels, sugar, soya milk, water and cinnamon. Stir well to disperse any lumps. Return the pan to the heat and bring to the boil whilst stirring, then continue stirring for a few minutes until the mixture thickens. Divide between 4 glasses, cover and put in the fridge until cold. Garnish with toasted pine kernels.

Spiced carrot halva   (Serves 4)

8oz/225g carrot, scraped and grated

5 fl.oz/150ml water

4oz/100g semolina

1oz/25g soft brown sugar

1oz/25g sultanas, chopped

1oz/25g walnuts, chopped

1 rounded teaspoon vegan margarine

¼ teaspoon ground allspice

8 fl.oz/225ml soya milk

Put the carrot and water in a saucepan and bring to the boil. Cover and simmer for about 10 minutes until soft, then remove from the heat and mash. Add the margarine and stir until melted. Mix the semolina with the sugar, sultanas, walnuts and allspice and add to the pan together with the soya milk. Combine well and return to the heat. Bring to the boil while stirring and continue stirring for a minute or two until the mixture is thick. Spoon into 4 glasses, cover and chill before serving.

Peach-stuffed pancakes   (Serves 6)

pancakes

4oz/100g plain flour

1 teaspoon easy-blend yeast

5 fl.oz/150ml soya milk

5 fl.oz/150ml water

vegan margarine

filling

1lb/450g firm peaches, stoned and chopped

1oz/25g sultanas

1oz/25g soft brown sugar

1 fl.oz/25ml fresh orange juice

1 teaspoon orange flower water

6 cloves

topping

fresh orange juice

1 tablespoon soft brown sugar

¼ teaspoon ground cinnamon

Mix the flour with the yeast. Warm the soya milk and water and add to the flour. Whisk well until no lumps remain. Cover and leave in a warm place for 1 hour.

Put all the filling ingredients in a saucepan and stir well. Bring to the boil and simmer for about 10 minutes until the fruit is soft.

Melt a little margarine in a hot non-stick 7 inch/18cm frying pan. Make 6 pancakes, using just over 2 tablespoonfuls of batter for each one. Keep the pancakes warm while making the next. Fold a pancake on individual dishes, fill them with some of the warm fruit mixture and sprinkle them with a little orange juice. Mix the sugar with the cinnamon and sprinkle over the top.

Dried fruit and bread pudding   (Serves 4)

4 thick slices of bread without crusts

vegan margarine

flaked almonds

4 tablespoons soya milk

2oz/50g dried figs

2oz/50g dried apricots

2oz/50g dried dates

2oz/50g raisins

10 fl.oz/300ml water

½ teaspoon ground cinnamon

Finely chop the figs, apricots and dates and put them in a pan with the raisins, water and cinnamon. Bring to the boil, cover and simmer for 15-20 minutes until the liquid has been absorbed and the mixture is thick. Stir occasionally to prevent sticking.

Spread one side of each slice of bread with margarine and cut the slices into cubes. Arrange a third of the cubes in a greased baking dish and top with half of the fruit mixture. Repeat these layers and finish with the remaining bread cubes. Spoon the soya milk over the top and sprinkle with flaked almonds. Bake in a preheated oven at 180°C/350°F/Gas mark 4 for 15-20 minutes until golden brown. Serve hot with yoghurt.

Melon sorbet   (Serves 4)

1lb/450g ripe melon flesh
2oz/50g sugar
1 dessertspoon rose water

Blend the ingredients until smooth. Pour into a freezerproof container, cover and freeze for 1 hour. Whisk the sorbet, then return it to the freezer for a few hours until just frozen. Should the sorbet freeze too hard, keep it at room temperature for 45 minutes before serving.

Orange rice pudding   (Serves 4)

2oz/50g ground rice
1oz/25g soft brown sugar
1 rounded dessertspoon vegan margarine
10 fl.oz/300ml fresh orange juice
10 fl.oz/300ml soya milk
1 teaspoon orange flower water
¼ teaspoon ground cloves
finely grated orange peel

Melt the margarine in a saucepan, add the ground rice and cloves and stir around for 30 seconds. Remove from the heat and stir in the orange juice and flower water. Bring to the boil and simmer while stirring for 1 minute, then take off the cooker and stir in the sugar and soya milk. Return to the heat and continue simmering for 3-4 minutes, stirring continuously, until the mixture is thick. Pour into 4 glasses, cover and put in the fridge until cold. Garnish with grated orange peel when serving.

BAKING

Some cakes and biscuits have traditionally been made for generations and are common to several countries in the Middle East, such as date and walnut ma'moul, sesame biscuits and fruited rice cake. These are sometimes served with strong black coffee to round off a meal, instead of a dessert. Various nuts, dates, figs and sesame seeds are all popular ingredients and the addition of flower waters to some recipes gives them a distinctive Middle Eastern flavour.

Date and walnut ma'moul   (Makes 9)

6oz/175g semolina

2oz/50g plain flour

2oz/50g vegan margarine, melted

approx. 4 tablespoons fresh orange juice

filling

4oz/100g dried dates, finely chopped

2 fl.oz/50ml water

¼ teaspoon ground cinnamon

1oz/25g walnuts, grated

Mix the semolina with the flour, add the melted margarine and stir well. Gradually add the orange juice and mix until everything binds together and forms a soft dough. Chill for 30 minutes.

Put the dates, cinnamon and water in a small pan and cook gently until the water has been absorbed and the dates are soft. Mash them with the back of a spoon until smooth, then add the walnuts and combine well. Take rounded dessertspoonfuls of the dough mixture and roll into balls in the palm of the hand. Form each ball into a little bowl. Divide the filling between the bowls and fold the dough over the filling to enclose, pinching it together to join. Put these little parcels on a greased baking sheet with the joins underneath and make an indent in the top of each one with a fork. Bake in a preheated oven at 170°C/325°F/Gas mark 3 for 20-25 minutes until just firm. Serve warm or cold.

Banana and almond bread

9oz/250g ripe bananas, peeled and mashed

6oz/175g self raising flour

2oz/50g ground almonds

2oz/50g vegan margarine

2oz/50g soft brown sugar

2 rounded tablespoons plain soya yoghurt

flaked almonds

Cream the margarine with the sugar, add the mashed bananas and ground almonds and mix well. Stir in the flour and yoghurt alternately, mixing well between additions. Spoon the mixture into a base-lined and greased 8 inch/20cm loaf tin and level the top. Sprinkle with flaked almonds, cover and bake in a preheated oven at 180°C/350°F/Gas mark 4 for 30 minutes, then uncover and bake for about 15 minutes until golden brown. Run a sharp knife around the edges of the tin and turn the bread out onto a wire rack. Allow to cool before cutting into slices.

Pistachio ring biscuits   (Makes approx. 20)

4oz/100g plain flour

2oz/50g pistachios, ground

2oz/50g vegan margarine

1½oz/40g soft brown sugar

1 dessertspoon rose water

2 tablespoons soya milk

Cream the margarine with the sugar and rose water. Work in the pistachios, then add the flour and soya milk and mix until a soft dough forms. Turn out onto a floured board and roll out to about ¼ inch/5mm thick. Cut into 2½ inch/6cm circles with a biscuit cutter and cut out the centre of each round with a 1 inch/2.5cm cutter. Transfer the rings to a greased baking sheet and gather up, re-roll and cut the remaining dough. Bake in a preheated oven at 180°C/350°F/Gas mark 4 for about 10 minutes until browned. Carefully slide onto a wire rack to cool.

Semolina and orange syrup slices   (Makes 8)

4oz/100g semolina

3oz/75g plain flour

2oz/50g vegan margarine

1oz/25g soft brown sugar

finely grated peel of 1 orange

5 fl.oz/150ml fresh orange juice

1 rounded teaspoon baking powder

chopped toasted flaked almonds

syrup

½oz/15g soft brown sugar

3 fl.oz/75ml fresh orange juice

1 dessertspoon orange flower water

Put the margarine and sugar in a pan and heat gently until melted. Remove from the heat and stir in the grated peel and semolina. Add the sifted flour and baking powder, alternating with the orange juice. Mix thoroughly, then spoon the mixture into a lined and greased 7 inch/18cm square baking tin. Spread out evenly and bake in a preheated oven at 180°C/350°F/Gas mark 4 for about 30 minutes until golden.

Bring the sugar, juice and orange flower water to the boil in a small pan. Stirring frequently, boil for about 5 minutes until a syrup forms. Pour this over the hot cake in the tin and leave to stand for 30 minutes. Sprinkle the top with toasted almonds and carefully remove the cake from the tin by lifting it out with the lining paper. Cut the square in half and each half into 4 equal slices and serve warm.

Sesame biscuits   (Makes approx. 14)

4oz/100g plain flour

2oz/50g vegan margarine

1oz/25g soft brown sugar

1 dessertspoon orange flower water

1 dessertspoon water

½oz/15g sesame seeds

Cream the margarine with the sugar, then work in the flour. Add the orange flower water and water and mix until everything binds together. Take heaped teaspoonfuls of the mixture and roll into balls. Roll the balls in the sesame seeds until coated all over, then flatten each ball into a biscuit shape and place on a greased baking sheet. Bake in a preheated oven at 180°C/350°F/Gas mark 4 for about 20 minutes until golden brown. Transfer to a wire rack to cool.

Spiced fruit bread rings   (Makes 8)

8oz/225g plain flour

2oz/50g dried dates, finely chopped

2oz/50g dried figs, finely chopped

1oz/25g soft brown sugar

1oz/25g vegan margarine, melted

½ sachet easy-blend yeast

½ teaspoon ground allspice

approx. 4 fl.oz/125ml soya milk, warmed

extra soya milk

sesame seeds

Mix the flour, yeast, sugar and allspice in a bowl. Stir in the dried fruits and melted margarine and gradually add the warmed soya milk until a soft dough forms. Knead well, then return to the bowl, cover and leave in a warm place for an hour until risen. Knead the dough again and divide it into 8 equal portions. Roll each portion into a ball, then make a hole in the centre and widen this to make ring shapes. Put these on a greased baking sheet and leave them in a warm place for 30 minutes. Brush the rings with soya milk and sprinkle them with sesame seeds. Bake in a preheated oven at 190°C/375°F/Gas mark 5 for about 15 minutes until browned. Serve warm.

Almond and semolina biscuits   (Makes approx. 14)

2oz/50g ground almonds

2oz/50g semolina

2oz/50g plain flour

2oz/50g vegan margarine

1oz/25g soft brown sugar

½ teaspoon almond essence

2 rounded tablespoons plain soya yoghurt

14 blanched almond halves

Cream the margarine with the sugar and almond essence. Mix the ground almonds with the semolina and flour, then work into the margarine mixture. Add the yoghurt and mix until a soft dough forms. Take rounded dessertspoonfuls of the mixture and roll into balls in the palm of the hand. Flatten each ball into a biscuit shape and put on a greased baking sheet. Press an almond half into the top of each biscuit and bake them in a preheated oven at 180°C/350°F/Gas mark 4 for about 15 minutes until golden. Carefully transfer to a wire rack to cool.

Walnut, fig and orange cake   (Serves 8)

6oz/175g self raising flour

4oz/100g dried figs, finely chopped

2oz/50g walnuts, grated

2oz/50g vegan margarine

1½oz/40g soft brown sugar

5 fl.oz/150ml fresh orange juice

1 dessertspoon orange flower water

½ teaspoon ground coriander

topping

½oz/15g walnuts, grated

½oz/15g soft brown sugar

3 fl.oz/75ml fresh orange juice

Gently heat the margarine and sugar until melted. Remove from the heat and stir in the walnuts, figs and orange flower water. Add the sifted flour and coriander alternately with the orange juice. Mix thoroughly, then spoon evenly into a lined and greased 7 inch/18cm diameter baking tin. Bake in a preheated oven at 180°C/350°F/Gas mark 4 for 25-30 minutes until golden brown.

Make the topping just before the cake is done. Put the walnuts, sugar and orange juice in a small pan and bring to the boil. Simmer for about 5 minutes, stirring frequently, until the mixture reduces down and thickens. Spread the topping evenly over the warm cake. Transfer the cake to a wire rack to cool before cutting it into wedges.

Fruited rice cake

6oz/175g plain flour

4oz/100g ground rice

3oz/75g vegan margarine

2oz/50g soft brown sugar

2oz/50g raisins

2oz/50g sultanas

2oz/50g dried dates, finely chopped

4 fl.oz/125ml fresh orange juice

1 rounded tablespoon finely grated orange peel

1 tablespoon date syrup

1 dessertspoon orange flower water

1 dessertspoon baking powder

¼ teaspoon ground cloves

¼ teaspoon ground cinnamon

sesame seeds

Put the raisins, sultanas, dates, orange peel, ground cloves and cinnamon, orange juice and flower water in a lidded container. Stir well, cover and leave for 2 hours.

Sift the flour and baking powder into a large bowl, add the ground rice and mix well. Rub in the margarine, then stir in the sugar. Combine the date syrup with the soaked fruit mixture and add to the dry ingredients. Mix very well, then spoon the mixture into a lined and greased 7 inch/18cm diameter cake tin. Sprinkle the top with sesame seeds and cover loosely with foil. Bake in a preheated oven at 180°C/350°F/Gas mark 4 for 25 minutes. Uncover and bake for 20-25 minutes more until browned. Carefully put on a wire rack and allow to cool completely before cutting.

Pistachio and yoghurt cake

4oz/100g plain flour

2oz/50g pistachios, ground

2oz/50g vegan margarine

2oz/50g soft brown sugar

6 fl.oz/175ml plain soya yoghurt

1 dessertspoon baking powder

1 teaspoon rose water

½ oz/15g pistachios, finely chopped

Cream the margarine with the sugar, add the yoghurt and rose water and mix until well combined. Stir in the ground pistachios, then add the sifted flour and baking powder. Mix thoroughly and spoon the mixture evenly into a lined and greased 7 inch/18cm diameter baking tin. Sprinkle the chopped pistachios on the top and press them in lightly with the back of a spoon. Bake in a preheated oven at 180°C/350°F/Gas mark 4 for 25-30 minutes until golden. Carefully turn out onto a wire rack to cool before cutting.

DRINKS

With temperatures soaring up to 40°C in some countries in the
Middle East, long, cool, refreshing drinks are the order of the day.
Fresh fruit sharbats are very popular thirst quenchers and they are
extremely easy to make. Glasses of ayran, a simple drink made from
blended plain yoghurt and water, are served at all meals and strong
black coffee is a favourite after dinner drink. A traditional welcome and
symbol of hospitality offered to guests in Arab homes is a cup of spiced
coffee served with a selection of dates.

Turkish ayran   (Serves 4)

8 fl.oz/225ml plain soya yoghurt
24 fl.oz/725ml iced water
ice cubes
fresh mint leaves

Blend the yoghurt with the water until frothy. Pour into 4 tumblers, add ice cubes and garnish with mint leaves.

Apricot and orange nectar   (Serves 4)

2oz/50g dried apricots, chopped
10 fl.oz/300ml water
18 fl.oz/550ml fresh orange juice
1 dessertspoon orange flower water
crushed ice
4 orange slices

Put the apricots and water in a saucepan and bring to the boil. Cover and simmer for 10 minutes. Allow to cool slightly, then transfer to a blender and add the orange juice and flower water. Blend until smooth and keep in the fridge for a few hours until cold. Stir well and pour into 4 glasses. Add crushed ice and garnish each glass with a slice of orange.

Melon sharbat   (Serves 4)

8oz/225g ripe melon flesh, chopped
20 fl.oz/600ml iced mineral water
1 dessertspoon sugar
melon balls

Blend the chopped melon, water and sugar until smooth. Pour into a jug and stir well, then pour out and garnish each glass with a few melon balls.

Minted lemonade   (Serves 4)

juice of 2 large lemons
24 fl.oz/725ml water
1½oz/40g sugar
4 rounded tablespoons chopped fresh mint
crushed ice
fresh mint leaves

Bring the lemon juice, water, sugar and chopped mint to the boil, stir and simmer for 5 minutes. Allow to cool and refrigerate until cold. Strain into glasses, add crushed ice and garnish with fresh mint leaves.

Pineapple and orange sharbat   (Serves 4)

8oz/225g pineapple flesh, chopped
8 fl.oz/225ml fresh orange juice
12 fl.oz/350ml water
1 dessertspoon orange flower water
crushed ice

Put the pineapple, orange juice, water and orange flower water in a blender and blend until smooth. Keep in the fridge until cold, then stir well. Pour into 4 glasses and add crushed ice.

Strawberry and orange sharbat   (Serves 4)

6oz/175g strawberries, chopped

16 fl.oz/475ml fresh orange juice

2 rounded tablespoons plain soya yoghurt

ice cubes

4 strawberries

Blend the chopped strawberries, orange juice and yoghurt smooth, pour into a jug and refrigerate. Serve the cold sharbat in glasses with ice cubes and garnished with a strawberry.

Iced minted tea   (Serves 4)

4 teaspoons tea leaves

4 teaspoons dried mint

2 teaspoons sugar

28 fl.oz/825ml boiling water

crushed ice

fresh mint leaves

Put the tea, dried mint, sugar and boiling water in a pot. Stir well, cover and refrigerate for a few hours until cold. Strain into glasses, add crushed ice and garnish with fresh mint leaves.

Ginger and lemon tea   (Serves 4)

½oz/15g root ginger, peeled and finely chopped

4 teaspoons tea leaves

1 tablespoon lemon juice

1 tablespoon sugar

28 fl.oz/825ml water

4 lemon slices

Bring the ginger and water to the boil, cover and simmer for 3 minutes. Add the tea leaves, lemon juice and sugar, stir well and continue simmering for 2 minutes more. Strain the tea into glasses and serve hot, garnished with lemon slices.

Gingered coffee   (Serves 4)

4 rounded teaspoons coffee granules

4 rounded teaspoons soft brown sugar

1 rounded teaspoon ground ginger

32 fl.oz/950ml water

Put the ingredients in a saucepan and stir well. Bring to the boil and simmer for 3 minutes before serving.

There are many other titles in this ongoing series of vegan cookery books. Already published are:

Vegan Dinner Parties

Vegan Baking

Vegan Barbecues and Buffets

A Vegan Taste of the Caribbean

A Vegan Taste of Italy

A Vegan Taste of India

A Vegan Taste of Mexico

A Vegan Taste of Thailand

A Vegan Taste of Central America

A Vegan Taste of East Africa

A Vegan Taste of Eastern Europe

Phone 01689 870437 for a free up-to-date catalogue of these and other publications of interest to vegans and vegetarians.